Henry Loomis Nelson

Our Unjust Tariff Law

A Plain Statement about High Taxes

Henry Loomis Nelson

Our Unjust Tariff Law
A Plain Statement about High Taxes

ISBN/EAN: 9783744766487

Printed in Europe, USA, Canada, Australia, Japan

Cover: Foto ©Suzi / pixelio.de

More available books at **www.hansebooks.com**

Our Unjust Tariff Law.

A Plain Statement

ABOUT

High Taxes.

BY

IENRY LOOMIS NELSON,

CLERK TO THE SPEAKER OF THE HOUSE OF REPRESENTATIVES.

WITH AN INTRODUCTORY LETTER

BY

HON. J. G. CARLISLE.

BOSTON:

CHARLES H. WHITING,

32 BROMFIELD STREET.

1884.

C. J. PETERS AND SON,
ELECTROTYPERS AND STEREOTYPERS,
145 HIGH ST., BOSTON.

PREFACE.

TⲎⲓⲥ book is intended to present the argument, as it stands to-day, in favor of a reduction of existing rates of duty, and of a tariff for revenue exclusively. The purpose is to state fairly the present positions of the protectionists and their opponents, and to show the merchant, and the men who work on farms, in shops, in factories, in offices, and in their studies, the evils inflicted upon the country by the protective system, and the benefits which were conferred by the low tariff which the country enjoyed between 1850 and 1860.

SPEAKER'S ROOM, HOUSE OF REPRESENTATIVES,
WASHINGTON, D. C., July 4, 1884.

HENRY L. NELSON, Esq.

DEAR SIR, — Learning that you have prepared and propose to publish a volume containing a condensed statement of the arguments in opposition to the protective system, and in favor of a revenue tariff, I desire to say that in my opinion such a work will, on account of the great importance of the subject to which it relates, be received as a welcome addition to what has already been done by the public press and our public men during the last few years. The question of revenue reform is now engaging the earnest attention of the people in every part of the country, and it is evident that the agitation must go on until the inequalities of our present system of taxation shall be removed, and the taxing power of the government restricted to its legitimate purposes. In order to secure these results there must be intelligent discussion of the whole subject in all its bearings upon the industrial and commercial interests of the country, and therefore every honest attempt to place within the reach of the people such facts and arguments as will enable them to understand the unjust operations of the existing system, and the advantages of a more liberal one, should receive the approbation and encouragement of all who desire to promote the welfare of those engaged in our various industries at home, as well as those employed in our foreign carrying trade.

Very respectfully yours,

J. G. CARLISLE.

OUR UNJUST TARIFF LAW.

I.

WHAT PROTECTION MEANS.

PROTECTION in this country means a tax levied on every merchant, working-man, farmer, and other consumer for the benefit of certain manufacturers.

The tax is indirect; it is paid, first, by the person who buys in a foreign country goods that are on the tariff list. In the end it is paid by the man who buys the goods for his own use. For example, if the government collects 55 per cent on a woollen coat which cost in England $10, the merchant who buys it and brings it here must pay for it $15.50, and when he sells it to the man who will wear it, he must charge him the $15.50 and the profit which he must get in order to pay the expenses of his store and his home and for savings. The $5.50 represents, speaking roughly, the difference between the price paid by the American who wears the coat and that paid by the Englishman who wears its mate.

There is no answer to this proposition. If the tax were not added to the price paid by the consumer, then there would be no "protection" about it.

This tax came to be called protective because it is supposed to make it profitable for Americans to engage in certain kinds of business, which they would not engage in if the law did not tax the people for their benefit.

For example: If A wants to be a woollen manufacturer, he first makes up his mind that the woollens that he will make will be too bad and too dear for the people of this country. Therefore he goes to the Congress and asks for "protection." He asks that the government shall make the price of foreign woollens so high that he can undersell the foreign manufacturers. The result is, that if an American buys the foreign woollen because he wants better cloth than is made in his own country, he must pay in the average 57.71 per cent more than an Englishman or Frenchman would be obliged to pay for it. The extra price goes to the government. If he buys American woollen, he pays more than it is worth, and this increased price goes to the manufacturer, in order that he may have a profitable business. If the American complains because the government takes away his savings to add to the savings of his neighbor the manufacturer, this manufacturer and his fellows say that the American is unpatriotic, because they have come to believe that the government was founded for their benefit.

This system was not always called protection. When our revolution came, it was called the "colonial system." By means of it Great Britain enabled those of her subjects living at home to make their several branches of business profitable at the expense of those of her subjects who lived in the colonies. The colonists were forced to trade with the mother country under severe penalties. One result of Great Britain's colonial system was the loss of her American colonies.

It was a universal heresy a hundred years ago, that trade ought to be governed and controlled by human laws; and that if, in commercial transactions, one nation was obliged to pay money to another nation, the first nation suffered a loss.

For example: If A is a baker and B is a tailor, and A buys his clothes of B, and B buys only a part or none of his bread of A, A pays for his clothes in money. He buys the clothes of B because he can get them cheaper of him than of any other tailor, while A charges more for his bread than B is willing to pay. Does A lose because he pays money to B instead of bread, selling his bread to those who are willing to pay more for it than B? This was the old doctrine about nations. Under this old doctrine it would have meant a loss if we sold our raw cotton to England for more than France would give, and paid money to France for silks. The doctrine of protection is a survival of the old ignorance and bigotry which considered it dangerous for nations to have commercial relations with each other.

When we had made peace with Great Britain, John Adams, Benjamin Franklin, and the other negotiators of our treaties with foreign powers attempted to secure an agreement for unrestrained trade; but the prejudices of the day were too strong, and the attempts failed. Then some of the States undertook to retaliate, for the purpose of making France and Great Britain come to terms. But the system did not work well, for the English ships unloaded in New York instead of Boston, and laughed at the little protection dodge. Still it was firmly fixed in the minds of most of the leading public men of a hundred years ago that it would be wise for the American people if Great Britain refused to permit them to sell what they raised from their soil in her dear markets, and to refuse, on their part, to purchase in her cheap markets. It was thus early that the true wisdom of protection asserted itself.

As soon as our present constitution was adopted, the agitation for protection was begun, and by that time the name " Protection " was employed.

Taxing commerce and labor and agriculture is a very indirect way to protect manufacturers; but it is the way it is done in this country. From the very first it was said, in speeches in Congress, and in laws enacted by Congress,

that the government must prevent the people of the United
States from trading too much, because money would be lost
if we bought what we needed too cheaply; that our people
must not engage too extensively in agriculture, but that
some of those who would naturally work on the farm must
be induced to work in the factory, in order that there might
be some one to eat up what was raised by those who per-
sisted in remaining farmers. The idea of the protectionists
was that we should make all the manufactured articles that
we used. Therefore in 1789 a law was enacted which put
a tax on imported articles, in order that their price might
be increased so much that Americans could make similar
articles and sell them for no more than the artificial price
fixed by the government. The theory was also that the
farmer ought to be invited to leave his fields and move into
a town, because he could earn more money in a factory than
on his land.   .

This theory makes the law of nature subordinate to the
law of man. The result of it is that a Congress of politicians enact statutes for the purpose of distributing labor
in diverse occupations, in order that the community may
enjoy greater wealth. These politicians assume that they
know what is best for men whose lives are devoted to making money; that men cannot be trusted to take care of their
own interests.

At first the protectionists were very modest. They did
not make demands; they preferred requests. The iron
industries of Pennsylvania wanted a little protection for a
very short time, in order that American working-men might
be educated sufficiently to enable them to compete with the
English operatives. As early as 1810, Mr. Gallatin, who
was Secretary of the Treasury, reported that the following
industries were "firmly established:" iron and manufactures of iron, manufactures of cotton, wool and flax, paper,

printing-types, books, etc. But this did not prevent a clamor for more protection. In fact the demands for protection increased the more protection was given.

For example: On manufactured cottons, not printed, stained, or colored, a duty of 15 per cent was imposed by the acts of 1797 and 1800; under the acts of 1804, 1807, and 1808 the duty was increased to 17½ per cent; the acts of 1812, 1813, 1815, and 1816 further increased the rate to 35 per cent. This indicates the advance of protection. It grew with what it fed on.

Presently the argument changed. Very early in the century it was announced by the protectionists that they believed in taxing imports without any view of raising revenue, but for the purpose of protecting manufacturers. This theory means nothing less than that if, of two men living in the same city, A desires to make cloth, and B desires to import similar cloth, the government ought to drive B out of business, by taxing what he desires to sell, in order that A may conduct his manufacturing business profitably.

This is substantially the present position of the protectionists. They say that they levy a tariff tax to prevent commerce, and to increase manufactures. This tax is paid by the person who buys the goods. If imported goods are bought, the importer adds the amount of duty paid by him to the other elements of cost. If domestic goods are bought, the manufacturer is enabled to charge the consumer the whole tariff duty in addition to the price he would have been obliged to accept if he had been forced to compete with the foreign goods.

The clamor of protected interests for more taxes on the people grew until 1824, when the rates of duty were increased so that the average rate was equal to 37 per cent. But even then the clamor did not cease. The manufacturers insisted that the people were not taxed enough, and that more taxes must be imposed in order that those who made blankets, and woollen goods, and hats, and trace-chains, and iron articles of all kinds, could gain more profit. Therefore, in 1828, the "tariff of abominations" was passed. Prof. Sumner says this tariff imposed an average tax of 41 per cent on the consumers of the country.

In 1833 reduction began, and it was a horizontal reduction, the law providing for a reduction of rates, every other year, by one-tenth of the excess over 20 per cent until 1841, and that in 1842 no rate of duty should be greater than 20 per cent.

In 1842 duties were again raised. In 1846 a tariff was passed that reduced duties to 25½ per cent, and in 1857 the duties were still further reduced to 20¼ per cent. From 1846 the country enjoyed great prosperity.

The Morrill Tariff Act of 1861 was the beginning of a new era of protection. Since that time the interests for whose benefit the people have been taxed have not ceased to clamor for more. The Morrill tariff lasted four months, and then tariff taxes were increased. Again in 1862 the taxes were raised, and again in 1864, 1865, 1866, and 1867. In 1870 there was a slight reduction of duties. In 1874, the average rate of duties was 38½ per cent.

In 1815 Mr. Clay asked for a tax of 25 per cent, saying that if this bounty were granted he believed that "three years would be sufficient to place our manufacturers on this desirable footing" [i. e. where their goods might be sold as cheaply as similar goods were sold abroad].

Mr. Clay is very often called "The Father of the American System." Those who make use of this expression mean that he is the originator of a system that taxes all the people of the country for the benefit of a few manufacturers. Mr. Clay believed that tariff taxes, like all other taxes, should be levied for the purpose of producing revenue for the country. If in doing this, he said, incidental protection can be afforded to home industry, he invoked every patriot to unite in effecting that object.

This is not the interpretation of the present generation of descendants of this "Father of the American System." . Senator Frye said, in 1882, "I am a protectionist from principle. If there were no public debt, no interest to pay, no pension list, no army and no navy to support, I still should oppose free trade and its twin sister, tariff for revenue only, and favor protective duties."

More recently still, Mr. Russell, a member of the Ways and Means Committee of the House of Representatives, announced in a speech in Congress that he belonged to the party of protection, and that that party would appeal to the people on its tariff policy, which was that taxes should be levied not only to support the government, but to "protect" (support) certain private citizens who desire to grow rich in the business of manufacturing, and who ask the government to enable them to realize their desire by compelling all their fellow-citizens to pay more for American goods than they would be obliged to pay for similar foreign goods ; and to prevent certain of their fellow-citizens from engaging in the business of importing such foreign goods.

Now, therefore, the meaning of protection is clear. It is that this government shall continue to lay a tax on the people for the support of the manufacturers. There were 50,155,783 people in this country, according to the last census, and only 3,837,112 of them were engaged in the work of manufacturing. When Mr. Morrill asked to have duties increased, in 1861, he said that the bill was a war measure. In 1864 he said again : — "This is intended as a war measure, a temporary measure, and we must, as such, give it our support."

In 1870 a number of those who now adopt the position laid down by the leading men of their party, that protection is right for the sake of protection, advocated a repeal of the war duties. Among these advocates of a freer trade were the late President Garfield and Senator Allison. About this time there was a reaction against the high tariff rates. The high rates were imposed in 1864, "as a necessary offset to internal revenue duties and as a temporary war tariff." Since the war four fifths of the internal taxes have been repealed, and still the duties remain as high as they ever were. Mr. Morrill said in 1870 : "Protection has here no legitimate claims, and it may be taken off whenever direct taxes are repealed and less revenue is desired." Two years before Mr. N. P. Banks, then a member of the Committee on Ways and Means of the House of Representatives, thought that the time had come when the duties must be taken off. Many New England manufacturers agreed with him, and they prepared a scheme of reduction in which they stated what their business could stand. Mr. Banks stated, on the floor of the House, that the manufacturers consented to a reduction of from 23 to 25 per cent.

But the reduction was not made. On the contrary, duties were increased, and three or four years ago there was another popular clamor for the lowering of tariff taxes. This time the country was given a commission, and revision was put off a year. The Commission reported that the best conservative business interests of the country demanded a reduction of duties of from 20 to 25 per cent. Congress passed a bill that reduced duties from 5 to 6 per cent, and now when the attempt is made to effect a reduction that shall fully satisfy the best conservative opinion of the country, the protectionists announce that they are in favor of maintaining the existing high rates, and of a tariff for the sake of the protection it affords. It is significant that they betray a consciousness of the growing weakness of their cause by a change of opinion as to the beneficiaries of their system. Formerly protection was for the purpose of building up manufactures; now they profess it is for keeping up the wages of American laborers.

From all that has been said it will be seen that there have been substantially two periods when the protective sentiment prevailed in Congress. The first was during the early days of the government, and the appeal was for the building up of manufactures. The second began with the war, and during this period a high protective tariff was fastened on the country for the purpose of raising a revenue made necessarily large by the demands of the war. The average duty before the revision was 40.52 per cent; the revision made it 38.14 per cent, according to a calculation made by the Bureau of Statistics.

From time to time this high tariff has been attacked, but from one cause or another it has escaped. After 1873 the protectionists begged that Congress should not disturb them while trade was depressed; in 1882 the plea was that business was too prosperous to permit of the "agitation of the tariff question." But the attack this time was in earnest, and the protectionists resorted to the commission scheme, under which a revision was made. Now that this revision is known to be unsatisfactory, and that protection must fight for existence, the position of its advocates is boldly announced. They are for protection for the sake of protection. They appeal to the country on the proposition that it is right to tax the people on an average about 40 per cent on every article in the long list of the tariff law, in order that certain manufacturers may add that 40 per cent to the price of their products.

II.

WHAT IS "A TARIFF FOR REVENUE ONLY"?

THERE is no doubt that a large part of the revenues of this country must continue to be raised from tariff duties. No one denies this, and no one desires to repeal all tariff taxes, unless it be some impracticable person whose desires and whose influence are in inverse ratio. The public men who are falsely called "free traders," believe that the system of tariff taxation should be changed gradually; that taxes should be at once reduced, but that the reduction should be made in such a way that no industry should unnecessarily suffer. If John Smith, for example, has invested $100,000 in a manufacturing business because the law promises to give him support and profit, no one desires to take his prop away suddenly. He will have plenty of time to look about for something — say, more enterprise and a larger market — to take the place of the taxes which have hitherto been imposed upon the people for his benefit.

The end to be reached by revenue reform is very clear. If a new start were to be made, those who are revenue reformers would object to any protective duties. What that means is this: They would advocate rates that would yield the amount of revenue needed by the government. Every tariff tax is of course a burden on commerce. If the average rate were what it was under the tariff of 1789, — 8½ per cent, — the manufacturer in this country would have just that much advantage over his French or English competitor. Mr. Russell, of Massachusetts, says that there is no such thing as incidental protection; that all protection that is not actually contemplated by the law is simply accidental. This is the necessary position of all protectionists

who favor the present high rate of duty. In insisting on
its maintenance they must demand protection for the sake
of protection. We know what the protectionists' idea of
protection is. It is to keep up taxes to the highest point
procurable from Congress. Therefore they oppose every
attempt at reduction, no matter how little the proposed
decrease of taxation may be. They certainly would not be
satisfied with a tax just sufficient to meet the expenditures
of the government, although — tax or no tax — the manufacturer in this country is protected against his European competitor by three thousand miles of ocean carriage, the cost
of which the importer must add to the price of his goods.
Therefore the manufacturer of this country has always some
protection against the foreigner. No duty can be collected
that does not raise the price somewhat. But what the
revenue reformer would insist on, were the whole question to
come before him as original, *i. e.*, if the country were about
to begin to make a tariff law, would be that the taxes, tariff
as well as direct, should be levied for public purposes exclusively.

Now, however, the question presented is different. The
protective tariff laws that have been enacted under one
pretext or another since 1860 have induced men to invest
money in manufacturing enterprises. These men, or many
of them, have already suffered serious losses by reason of
the very law for the continuance of which they beg; but
there is no doubt that many manufacturers would be finan-
cially ruined by the sudden and entire removal of the protective prop. Therefore no one proposes to take away alto-
gether, and at once, what they receive from the people,
because it has been given to them by the representatives of
the people, who were, it is true, filled with the vague and
unwholesome doctrine of protection, but who, nevertheless,
were really the representatives, and whose action had been

indorsed by the voters, so far as their retention in Congress, for many prominent reasons, can be considered an
indorsement of a dogma that has not been made prominent
at all.

The action of the protective system is almost invariable.
Men of large capital invest in a business. It may be in
manufacturing, or it may be in wool-growing. They find
either that they cannot make the business pay at all, or that
it does not pay as great an interest as they think ought to
be returned to them from their investment. They go to
Congress for assistance. Sometimes they send agents bearing petitions; sometimes they secure the election to Congress of some one or two of their own number. Finally
they obtain protection, and they are enabled to add to the
price of the articles which they manufacture or grow from
10 to 100 per cent. The result is that, for a time, the business becomes enormously profitable, and a large number of
other people engage in it. Some of these people have little
capital. In the course of time comes the natural end of an
unduly profitable business, of a disproportionately stimulated
trade. If the business is wool-growing, too many farmers
raise sheep; if it be manufacturing, too many mills are
built. The result can be foreseen by everyone except
those whose money is invested, and they are blinded by the
statute book, in which is printed the promise that the government will provide them with profits out of the pockets of
the people. The market becomes glutted with wool, or
with the products of the mills, and the price falls. It con-
tinues to fall because there is no demand for the goods,
which cannot be sent abroad to seek a foreign market, as
the general system of protection has increased the cost of
production so much that competition with foreign products
in their own markets, is out of the question. Then the small
farmers or manufacturers fail, while the capitalists close their

mills, or lock up their wool and wait. While they are
waiting their laborers go without employment, and the
farmer who raise produce suffers again because the working-men have no money with which to pay for the food
needed by them and their families.

For example: A and B buy 10,000 sheep and determine
to grow wool. This is in 1860, before the wool tariff was
enacted. They do not make as much money as they think
they ought to make, and they get a tax of from 5 to 25 per
cent levied on their fellow citizens in order that their business may be rendered profitable. The tax is levied on
foreign wools and increases their price, so that the price
on American wool may be also increased. The increase
makes the business profitable, and the farmer neighbors of
A and B, who are not so rich as the wool-growers, determine that they will embark in the business into which the
government has entered as a partner. So they buy 50 or
100 sheep each and greatly increase the aggregate number.
This is all supposed to occur in a very simple and small
country. Soon there is more wool in the market town than
the people want. The poorer farmers cannot afford to remain without the money which they had expected to
receive from their crops. They therefore sell for what
they can get and are ruined. In the meantime A and B
are waiting and refusing to sell their wool. They are rewarded in the end by receiving a high price for their product, their poorer contemporaries having been driven out of
competition, and the demand for wool having revived. But,
in the meantime, the whole company, rich and poor, prosperous and bankrupted, go to the government for more
"protection," and the government kindly levies another tax
on the people for the benefit of those who persist in raising
sheep for their wool, when they ought to be growing grass
or grain.

This is the old and familiar story of protective tariffs. It is recognized as familiar by all who are acquainted with the subject. The revenue reformers believe that not only has the government no right to tax the people for the benefit of private persons, but that business fostered in this artificial way has an unnatural growth. It may reach prosperity, as many of our manufacturing concerns have attained a solid basis, but the advance is through disaster, the loss of capital, the crushing out of many men who are unable to stand the ups and downs of an unnatural growth and expansion of business, and the destruction of other legitimate enterprises. Under the first laws there are commercial disasters, but such disasters in a "protected" country are not only the more numerous, but the more difficult to recover from.

It is for the sake of preventing the crushing out of well-established industries, as well as of those that are still struggling for existence, that revenue reformers are desirous of reaching their end slowly. They are not dealing with an original question, but they are applying a remedy to a body politic that is, economically, very ill. They believe that a wholesome system of taxation confines the revenue to the needs of the government. They are strongly opposed to a system that puts a tax on foreign goods into the treasury, and at the same time permits a private citizen to levy another tax for his own benefit on his own product. They propose to give the country such a system in the end; but they propose to reach that end conservatively and with the least possible injury to existing interests.

The revenue reformers begin by asserting that the existing rates of duty are too high; not merely that they are protective. They say that many of them are prohibitory, so that no revenue is derived from them. The protectionists will answer, if they are honest in their assertions in favor of their system, that they are glad of this; that they want foreign goods kept out of our markets entirely, so that our own citizens may make whatever we need, no matter what may be the cost to the consumer.

For example: Suppose that A and B are alone in the world. A makes clothes rapidly and well, and B is a farmer and produces food. Naturally, one would suppose that A would make B's clothes and take B's food products in exchange, but they are too wise to obey the laws of nature, so they adopt the policy of protection. A proposes to raise all he wants to eat himself as well as to make all the clothes he wears, and B insists on doing likewise. Now if A made clothes for both, and B raised food for both, each man would work a rational number of hours every day, and the two might have a good deal of leisure which they might spend in pleasure or intellectual improvement, as they chose. This leisure is wealth; for what more can wealth bring to its possessors? As it is, however, they have enslaved themselves. When they get through their work in the fields, they cannot sit down to rest; they must go to work to make clothes for themselves.

But to return. The revenue reformers say that the rates of the present tariff are too high for any purpose, protective or otherwise. They say that the tax levied by the government for the benefit of manufacturers gives to some of the favored class an unduly great profit. They are assisted by the law not only to exist, but to attain an enormous prosperity at the expense of people who do not desire any benefit from their existence, but upon whom they rest as a burden.

This is the immediate proposition before the country. The question is not, Shall we have free trade? No one wants that now or ever, if by free trade is meant the repeal of all customs duties. The question is, Shall we begin the work of establishing a rational system of taxation, by cutting down the rates that are confessed, even by protectionists, to

be too high. The manufacturers themselves confessed it in
1868, through their spokesman in the House of Representatives, Mr. N. P. Banks. The senators and representatives
who are now in favor of maintaining the present rates confessed it in 1870 in Congress. The whole body of protectionists confessed it when they voted for the bill creating a
tariff commission. And that commission confessed it in the
following language: —

> "Early in its deliberations the commission became convinced that
> a substantial reduction of tariff duties is demanded, not by a mere
> indiscriminate popular clamor, but by the best conservative opinion
> of the country, including that which has in former times been most
> strenuous for the preservation of our national industrial defences. . . .
> "The average reduction in rates, including that from the enlargement of the free list and the abolition of the duties on charges and
> commissions, at which the commission has arrived, is not less, on
> the average, than 20 per cent, and it is the opinion of the commission
> that the reduction will reach 25 per cent."

The revenue reformers say that the revision was a sham.
In his closing speech on the motion to strike out the enacting clause of his bill, Mr. Morrison exposed the jugglery of
the report of the conference committee, which was passed
by both Houses of Congress, and is now the law. He
said: —

> "Out of one of the rates fixed or clauses made in the last tariff bill
> by the gentleman from Ohio and his associates, experts who have made
> all the tariffs since 1860, I am told 15,000 protests have already come
> and 15,000 lawsuits may follow. So it would appear that there is
> something defective, more or less imperfect, in all tariff bills. And
> dread confusion haunts the gentleman from Ohio because the duty on
> grindstones is to be lowered. He came confused from yonder conference-room, where he was a member of the conference committee,
> to the confusion of all taxpayers. The office and duty of a conference
> is to adjust the difference between the two disagreeing Houses. This
> House had decided that bar-iron of the middle class was to pay $20
> a ton; the Senate that it was to pay $20.16 a ton. The gentlemen of

the conference, including the gentleman from Ohio, reconciled this difference — how ? By raising bar-iron above both House and Senate to $22.40 a ton. The Tariff Commission, at the end of its deliberations, reported that the tariff on iron ore should be 50 cents a ton. The Senate said that it should be 50 cents a ton. The House said it should be 50 cents a ton. Gentlemen of the conference committee, including the gentleman from Ohio, neither indolent nor wanting in capacity of a kind, reconciled the agreement of the House, Senate, and Tariff Commission into a disagreement, where there was none, and made the duty on ore 75 cents a ton. The gentlemen of the conference did a similar service for the great corporation of corporations, the Iron and Steel Association, by giving it a tax of $17 on steel rails, which the House fixed at $15 and the Senate at $15.08 per ton. In all this there is no confession of want of capacity, but an exhibition of it which commends itself to the gentleman from Ohio. It is such an exhibition of talent and special fitness as in Ohio would be a breach of public trust and drive him from an honorable profession. Here it is statesmanship. It gives bounty to corporations and royalty to mine-owners. It adds to the burdens of the people, who are mocked with the pretence that it protects labor. The more of such evidences of capacity as were exhibited in that conference, of which the gentleman from Ohio was a distinguished member, that might be shown in this horizontal bill, the more infamous it would be, and the less support it ought to have. These gentlemen who come here from Iowa, Wisconsin, and Michigan, pledged to abate something from taxes taken from the people to go into a treasury already full, come as the representatives of a people who believe the Tariff Commission scheme was a sham and a cheat, devised to maintain and not to reduce taxes. And now they are here, and the chief financial officer of the government tells them (whether it is a cheat or not) that this scheme has not reduced taxes as it was promised they should be reduced — as all advocates of the commission plan promised they should be reduced.

The average rate of duty under the old law was 40.52 per cent; under the present law it is about 38.14. If the revised law had really reduced the rates as much as the commission recommended, the average rate would now be 30.39. This was the rate admitted to be just by every protectionist who favored the commission's report, and not one friend of the protected interests was heard to protest against the

measure. It would be interesting to know how many men
in the country, and who, were acquainted with the fact that
the revised law would not reduce taxation. This, however,
is now certain, that when they know that taxation has not
been reduced to the point which they admitted to be just,
they refuse to consent to a further reduction which would
make taxation more nearly what was promised in the names
both of the Tariff Commission and of the Ways and Means
bills in the Forty-seventh Congress. For it should be recol-
lected that the Ways and Means Committee of the present
Congress reported a bill to the House of Representatives
which proposed to carry out the promises made in the last
Congress; but the average rate of the Morrison bill was 31.17
per cent, almost one per cent more than the rate admitted
to be high enough by the protectionists only a year before.

The revenue reformers say that when a man buys a dollar's worth of cotton goods, 40 to 56 cents of it is too much
to pay to the government; that when a woman buys woollen
stuff for a dress, 68 cents is too much to give the government; that 50 cents is too much to pay on every dollar's
worth of sugar that goes into family consumption. The
protectionists insist that these high taxes shall be maintained. This is the present status of the controversy. The
revenue reformers say that the government ought to begin
the reduction of tariff taxation; the protectionists say that
the present taxes ought to be maintained.

III.

SOME OF THE EVILS OF THE PRESENT TARIFF

THE present tariff law was enacted March 3, 1883. The pretence was that it was not only a revision of the law as it then stood, but a reform in the direction of lower duties. This is not true, as the statement of a few facts will show. In the first place, as already shown, the average rate of duty collected under the old law was 40.52 per cent; under the present law it is 38.14 per cent.

Most of the articles consumed by those who are not rich are taxed more heavily under the new than under the old law. And some of this increased taxation was very cunningly devised.

For example: The rate on the coarsest kinds of plain cottons, worth a little more than 12 cents a yard, was reduced from 39.91 per cent to 19.95 per cent; on these goods bleached, the rate was reduced from 48.81 to 31.07 per cent; if dyed, colored, stained, painted, or printed, the rate was reduced from 47.24 to 28.05. These prints are worth about 16 cents a square yard. On prints of a little higher quality, worth a little more than 16 cents, the rate was reduced from 56.19 per cent to 30.88 per cent. Of the prints of the first kind there were imported in 1883 only 390,906 square yards. Most of the goods of this quality which are consumed here are manufactured in this country. But when cotton goods that make the best wear of the poorer people are reached, there is an increase of rate from 35 to 40 per cent. Of prints that are worth more than 20 cents a square yard, there were imported, in 1883, 4,841,664 yards. All the laces that are used by people who are not rich are of cotton, and on these and embroideries, insertings, trimmings, lace window curtains, cotton damask, hemmed handkerchiefs, and cotton velvet, the rate was increased by the revised law from 35 to 40 per cent. By a change in the schedules which may or may not have been understood by the manufacturers, the duties on certain grades of cotton goods were greatly increased from the old ad valorem rate of 35 per cent. The rate on black crinoline lining, for example, was increased to an average of 111 per cent; and that on tarlatans to an average of 103 per cent. On one grade of linings the rate is as high as 148 per cent, and on one grade of tarlatan it reaches 153 per cent.

The rate on dress goods made in part of wool, valued at more than 20 cents a square yard, was reduced from 8 cents and 40 per cent to 7 cents and 40 per cent; this changed the ad valorem rate from 68.45 to 64.89 per cent. Therefore if the wife of a farmer or working-man now desires to purchase a dress of stuff partly wool, worth in England 25 cents a yard, she must pay in this country 42 cents; the 17 cents going as a tax to the government or as a bounty to the manufacturer. But it is well known that the best wear of people who are not rich is "all-wool" goods. The rate of duty on these goods was increased by the revision from 8 cents and 40 per cent to 9 cents and 40 per cent. No one can tell how much this increased the ad valorem rate, for it stopped importations. A person who buys American all-wool dress goods, like those which could be bought abroad for 40 cents a yard, must pay at least 62 cents a yard for them in this country.

In the metal schedule there are many curiosities. Cast-iron vessels, plates, stove plates, andirons, sadirons, tailors' irons, hatters' irons, and castings of iron, used to pay a rate of duty of 32.64 per cent; under the revised and reformed law the rate is 104.01 per cent.

The crockery trade sells painted and printed earthen and

stone ware, which is very cheap, and is used by the poorest people in the country. Some of this crockery is so cheap that it is made for the southern negro trade. Every one has seen the children's plates, with an alphabet around the rim, and a picture in the centre. This picture is first printed and then painted, the painting being very rude, and done in the crudest way by women and children. Forty per cent on this class of work was not enough for these revisers, who thought that the conservative opinion of the country demanded lower duties; so they increased the rate to 60 per cent, and classified this coarse ware with china, porcelain, parian and bisque, that was ornamented. Plain china, porcelain, parian, and bisque, which can be afforded by the rich only, pays a lower duty and bounty than the stone cups of the poor, and even plain white stone ware pays as much as plain white porcelain. And yet the country is assured by men who are generally considered honest that the present tariff is for the benefit of American working-men.

So much for the pretended reform made by the revision. There are other features of the law that are interesting to people who work with their hands for a living. Ready-made clothing pays 40 cents a pound and 35 per cent. A rich man sends to a London tailor for clothes, for which the charge is $50; a poor man buys in this country a suit which he could buy abroad for $20. Assuming that each suit weighs five pounds, the rich man pays the government a tax of 39 per cent, while the poor man pays the American manufacturer a bounty of 45 per cent, and he pays $29 for what ought to have cost him $20. If a poor man buys a coarse woollen blanket, worth 54 cents per pound, he pays 60 per cent to the government or the manufacturer. If a rich man buys a blanket worth $1.50 a pound, he pays no more tax or bounty than the poor man. The average rate on the low-priced flannels, blankets, wool hats, etc., is 68.77 per cent; on the highest-priced, 62.08.

A drugget or blocking pays a duty of 72.18 per cent; but an Axminster carpet pays only 55.52 per cent.

Halter-chains, trace-chains, and fence-chains, that are used by the farmers, and are worth about five cents a pound, pay about 47.14 per cent, while finer chains pay 45.41. The finest salt pays less than 40 per cent, while the coarse salt used for preserving meats, feeding cattle, etc., pays a little less than 64½ per cent.

Sugar, which must be used by every one, pays a duty of from 50 to 68.20 per cent; and this highest, duty is on a grade of sugar that can be consumed without refining, and the use of which, were the duty lower, might therefore save the poorer people of the country an immense sum of money every year.

But the protectionists object to reducing the rates of duty. They say that to do so would lower wages. In due time this will be demonstrated to be arrant nonsense or deliberate falsehood. Protection to American industries was first granted for the purpose of giving a profit to the capitalists who invested their money in manufacturing enterprises. Wages must be higher in this country than in England so long as agricultural land is as cheap as it is, and agricultural labor as remunerative. The protectionists threaten the working-men with reduced wages if they vote to relieve themselves from burdensome taxes; but, while they are making their threats, they do lower wages, even under a protective system, with whose generous bounty they sometimes profess themselves satisfied. There is no better protected industry than that of iron and steel, and yet its revived prosperity, which began in 1879 with the general financial revival of the country, lasted only three years. The report of the American Iron and Steel Asso-

ciation shows that nearly all the mills closed in 1882, and
that during the four months when they were idle the operatives were the losers. The prices of iron and steel did not
advance because there was enough material on hand to
supply the demand. This means that under the artificial
stimulus of protection the mills produced more than was
needed. It was simply a new illustration of a well-established fact. Protection always leads to over-production,
and when that happens the capitalists stop expenses, sell
their surplus, and meanwhile the operatives starve or get
into debt. Judging from the reports that come from the
iron regions at this writing, the iron and steel industry is in
as bad condition as it was two summers ago, when nearly
all the rolling-mills of Pittsburg and the West were closed
for four months.

The statistics relative to hoop iron, bar iron, iron rails,
sugar, and molasses, for 1880, serve admirably to show the
workings of the present tariff, and the price paid by the
American people to sustain what protectionists call the
"American system." In 1880 there were produced in this
country, hoop (band and scroll) iron to the value of
$6,094,484; and there was imported $720,903.82 worth.
The domestic product cost $62.67 a ton; the imported ar-
ticle cost $45.56. The rate of duty was $31.66. The cost
of the foreign iron, with freight added, would have been
$48.06, so that the consumer was obliged to pay $14.61
bounty on every ton of American hoop iron used by him;
and the total bounty paid by American consumers amounted
to $1,414,876.22. From these figures it will be seen that
for every dollar paid to the treasury as duty, the American
manufacturer received $2.82 bounty.

In the same year the production of bar iron in this
country amounted to $35,302,431; the imports to $3,111,-
218.43. The domestic article was valued at $53.33 a ton,

the foreign at $43.33. Duty was $22.86, and the cost per
ton of foreign iron, with freight added, $45.83. The bounty
of the manufacturer was $7.40 per ton, and the bounty paid
by consumers on domestic production was to duty received
by the Treasury as $2.99 is to $1.

The domestic production of iron rails was $20,978,637;
imports, $1,635,980; cost, $44.93 and $31.10; duty, $15.68;
cost of foreign rails, freight added, $33.60; bounty, $11.33;
ratio of bounty to duty, $6.41 to $1.

The foreign sugar imported into this country in 1880 was
worth $68,052,639.55; the average duty per pound was 2.44
cents. The value of the domestic product was $13,191,-
200.02. The value of the imported molasses was $8,978,-
008.50; of the domestic product, $3,528,770.51. On the
total importation of sugar and molasses, $77,030,648.05;
the duty was $42,203,915.49; while the bounty on the do-
mestic product was $5,616,503.96. For $94,000,000 worth
of sugar and molasses the people of the country paid
$142,000,000.

These are some of the enormities of the present tariff.
The man who consumes the products of our own mills, or
who buys the imported products of foreign mills, pays for all
his cottons an average of 38.29 per cent more than the goods
are worth; on his wife's woollen shawl, 65.83 per cent; on
his blankets, wool hats, flannels, knit goods, etc., about 67 per
cent; on his carpets, from 40 to 70 per cent; for all the
sugar his family consumes, about 50 per cent; for the iron
vessels of his kitchen, about 104 per cent; for his knives
and forks, 35 per cent; for needles, 25 per cent; for the pens
with which he writes, 50 per cent; for his tin utensils, 45
per cent; for his wooden furniture, 35 per cent; for his
other woodenware, the same; for his brown earthenware,
25 per cent; for his white stoneware, 55 per cent; for the
slate and pencils of his children, 30 per cent; for preserve

jars, 35 per cent; for his common window-glass, from 66 to 74 per cent; for his provisions, an average of 21 per cent.

Suppose a man in moderate means wants to furnish a house. How much, under the present tariff law, must he pay for $1,000 worth of furniture? Here is a table showing, in the first column of figures, the worth, and in the second the price to be paid after the tariff has added the duty, or bounty : —

	Worth.	Price.
Wooden Furniture	$700.00	$945.00
Carpets	200.00	298.83
($125 Tapestry Brussels and $75 two- ply ingrain)		
White Stoneware	40.00	62.00
Brown Earthenware	10.00	12.50
Iron Kitchenware	15.00	30.60
Tin " "	15.00	21.75
Woodenware	10.00	13.50
Cutlery	10.00	13.50
	$1,000.00	$1,397.68

A bounty of $398 is paid by the consumer, and the same fate follows him through life. He pays more for all that goes to the feeding and clothing of his family. For every $100 worth of cottons, he pays, on an average, $138.29; for a $10 woollen shawl he pays $16.58; for $20 worth of flannels he pays about $33.40; $10 worth of sugar costs him $15, and so on through the long list of taxed articles. When he is born his sponsors pay $14 for his $10 silver mug, and when he dies his executors take from his widow $95 to pay for a $50 monument.

The protectionists say that they will not remedy these evils; that they will not consent to any reduction whatever. In the last session of Congress they took the position that they would not debate the question, they would not consider it; and later, when they were forced to consider it,

they refused to try, by offering amendments, to take any
steps to make a good bill. The refusal of the protectionists to
vote for the Morrison bill is conclusive evidence that they
propose to do nothing for the relief of the consumers. They
refused the most moderate reductions, — to cut down the
duty on cotton and cotton goods from 38.29 per cent to 31.50 ;
on hemp, jute, and flax goods, from 28.04 to 24.61 ; on wool
and woollens, from 57.71 to 46.43 ; on metals, from 35.19 to
29.81 ; on books, papers, etc., from 21.67 to 18.51 ; on sugar
and molasses, from 43.59 to 34.87 ; on tobacco, from 72.70 to
58.16 ; on wood and woodenware, from 33.98 to 29.35 ; on
earthenware and glassware, from 53.16 to 44.12 ; on provisions, from 24.17 to 21.01 ; on sundries, from 25.46 to 22.60 ;
on chemical products, from 37.11 to 31.40.

If they will not make such moderate reductions of taxes,
what is to be expected from them? But at any rate the
country is afforded a view of the standard of taxation that
is deemed necessary for the fostering of these aged infant
industries. The conclusion that must be reached is that the
protectionists propose to keep all the benefits they have
received, and to secure all other possible advantages. The
tax was first granted to meet the necessities of the war ; it
has been preserved because it is said to be needful to tax
the people for the benefit of a few manufacturers ; and now
that the government's surplus reaches to the neighborhood
of $100,000,000, the protectionists refuse to yield a cent
of their enormous bounty.

IV.

WHAT PROTECTION MEANS TO THE FARMER.

OF the 17,392,099 persons engaged in wealth-producing occupations in 1880, 7,670,493 were agriculturists, farmers, and farm laborers. Almost half the working population of the country, therefore, drew their sustenance from the soil. The amount of capital in farms, agricultural implements, and live-stock is very large. In 1880 it was $12,104,081,440, while the capital invested in manufactures was only $2,790,-272,606. What does protection do for the farmer?

In the first place it increases the cost of everything he is obliged to buy. How much more his clothing, his groceries, his household furniture and utensils cost, has already been shown. His agricultural implements cost him at least half as much again as they ought, because of the duties which the manufacturers are obliged to pay. The tariff adds 25 per cent to the cost of transporting his products to market. In return he receives a duty that amounts to about 25 per cent on his leading staples, and which he does not need.

The American farmer is the one producer in this country who is compelled to sell in a foreign market. Wheat is so largely produced that our own population cannot consume it. The surplus of the wheat product in 1883 was more than 100,000,000 bushels. This surplus is sold to Europe, so that American wheat competes with the wheat of the world. Its price is regulated by the markets of Liverpool. In determining the price at which he will sell his goods, the manufacturer can add to the cost of foreign-made goods the freight charge across the ocean, and the duty; but the farmer must deduct freight charges, and must meet the European wheat growers on their own ground. The result is that the price paid for wheat in Liverpool determines the price paid in this country. The 20 cents a bushel duty, therefore, does no good; it is never collected by the farmer as a bounty. This truth about wheat comes home to the American farmer now as it has never come before. The increase in the wheat product of India has become astonishing. Last year 40,000,000 of bushels of wheat were exported from India. The result is that the exportation of American cereals has greatly decreased, and the price of American wheat has fallen below 80 cents a bushel.

Now the question which the American farmer has to answer is, Can he go on paying taxes for the benefit of his neighbor, the manufacturer, while he is forced to sell in the cheapest market of the world? Can he afford to burn his candle at both ends? What he buys costs him more than similar articles cost in Europe, and yet he receives per bushel just what his English competitor receives, and just what is received by his Indian competitor, whose clothes consist of a single yard of cotton. The average farmer is not a rich man. As the value of the farm products of the United States in 1880 was $2,213,402,504, while the persons engaged in farm labor numbered 7,670,493, it follows that the average income of farmers and farm laborers was $289 a year. To the ordinary cost of living must be added the $450,000,-000 which the farmers pay annually in taxes and bounties for the maintenance of the business of their manufacturing neighbors. Can the farmers afford the luxury?

The pretence of the protectionists is that the establishment of manufactures furnishes a home market. On the theory of the protectionists there is only one kind of a home market that is worth anything. It is a market from which all foreign competition is excluded. That is the kind of home market the protected manufacturers desire for themselves. In their speeches at the last session of Congress, they said that they favored the continuance of the present high rate of taxation in order that our people might be supplied with everything of American manufacture. The main object of the protectionists of the present day is to prohibit the importation of foreign goods. In other words, the leaders of the protectionists hold that it is right for the government to tax the people in order to prevent revenue. Therefore, when a perfect tariff law shall be made, the large revenue now collected by the custom houses will go entirely into the pockets of the manufacturers, and the government must be supported by direct taxation; internal revenue taxes must be increased rather than diminished.

But the American farmer cannot have this kind of a home market. He produces too much for the country, and, in the natural order of things, production must increase rather than diminish. The manufacturers' promise of supplying an adequate home market has not been kept. Half the people of the country pay every year $450,000,000 for a market which they do not get, and for higher prices which they do not realize. How much did this market demand in 1880, the census year? The people engaged in manufacturing, with all those employed in mechanic and mining pursuits added, consumed only $335,000,000 worth, while the producers were obliged to sell abroad $685,961,091 worth. The only result of the protective system to the farmer is to increase the cost of living.

Moreover, statistics show that the proportion of our crops consumed at home has been greater under low tariffs than under high tariffs. Under the low tariff of 1846, in the census year 1850, the total cereal production was 867,453,967 bushels, of which we consumed at home 851,502,312 bushels, and exported 15,951,655, or 1.9 per cent. In 1860, under the still lower tariff of 1857, the production was 1,239,039,-945 bushels, of which the home market purchased 1,216,-

084,810 bushels, and 22,955,135 bushels, or 1.8 per cent, were exported. In 1870, under a high protective tariff, the total production was 1,629,027,600 bushels; 1,571,737,179 bushels were consumed in this country, and 57,290,521 bushels, or 3.50 per cent, were sent abroad. From 1850 to 1860 the production of grain increased 45.1 per cent, while the exports increased 43.9 per cent, while under a high tariff law, from 1860 to 1870, production increased 31.4 per cent, while the exports increased 149.50 per cent.

More than 80 per cent of the exports of this country are of agricultural products. There is no complaint made by protectionists because the farmers are obliged to compete with the freed serfs of Russia or the laborers of India. On the contrary, our farmers are asked to go on competing, and at the same time to put their hands in their pockets and pay a bounty to the manufacturers, in order that their brother working-men who prefer to labor in the mills may not be obliged to compete with the British operatives. It is not true that the wages of our own operatives will ever be governed by the wages paid in Great Britain; nor is it true that the protectionists desire high tariff taxes for the laborer, for they are looking entirely after the interests of capital. But, leaving all that aside for the time, is it fair to ask the American farmer to compete with lately emancipated serfs and Indian ryots and half-naked Africans, and at the same time to tax himself to prevent the operatives of mills from coming into competition with the skilled laborers of Great Britain?

It has been shown that the home market which the protectionists have promised has not been furnished by the establishment of manufactures; that out of their slender incomes the farmers of the country are forced to contribute to the manufacturers $450,000,000 annually. What is the result, to the manufacturers, of this contribution, and what to the farmers? In 1880 the capital invested in manufactures was $2,790,272,606; the product was $5,369,579,191. Deducting from this the value of materials used and the wages paid, we have a gross profit of $1,024,801,847, or between 36 and 37 per cent. It is estimated that the gross profits of the farmers is $1,436,944,067, which is between 11 and 12 per cent on the capital, $12,104,081,430, invested in the business of agriculture. It is strange that a business paying the small return should be taxed to sustain enterprises whose profits exceed the profits of its benefactor three times. The American farmer is the victim of a bad system, and a deluded victim whenever he votes for a protectionist for Congress.

V.

WHAT PROTECTION MEANS TO THE WORKING–MAN.

JUST now it is the burden of the protection song that American labor would be degraded if the tariff were reduced. On the contrary the laborers of the country would be benefited. It is perfectly clear that taxing working-men does not benefit them unless at the same time their incomes are increased more than enough to make up the tax. The average tax imposed by the existing tariff is 39 per cent, but, as has been shown, the working-man pays 50 per cent tax on his sugar, over 60 per cent on some of his woollens, about 40 per cent on his cottons, 55 per cent on his ready-made clothes, and so on. Is there any return made for this by the tariff? Are his wages increased more than the cost of living? If they are not, then protection is an injury to the working-man.

In the first place the large majority of working-men do not

labor for protected industries. The only man who can give larger wages by reason of the tariff is a manufacturer who receives a bounty from the tax imposed upon the consumers. The fund from which wages are paid must be increased if wages themselves are to be greater. This increase is given up to the manufacturer. It has been shown that the farmer suffers from the exactions of the tariff. All that he buys is dearer for it, and all that he sells is as cheap as can be. The laborer for the farmer must suffer with his employer, and he suffers so much that the average annual income of all workers in agriculture, including employer and working-man, is only $289. Of course the farm laborer gets nothing but increased taxation from the tariff. He pays more than he ought for his clothes, for his boots and shoes, for his blankets, for his hats, for his provisions, for his rent, for everything which he must have to sustain life; and as his employer's income is decreased by his share of the $450,000,000 annually paid by the farmers to support their richer manufacturing neighbors, he is obliged to sustain, in reduced wages, even more than his own share of the burdens of tariff taxation.

It is equally true that the working-men in the mechanical industries receive no benefit from the tariff. The protectionist who would assert that a carpenter or a mason receives more wages because the cotton, woollen, and iron manufacturers are the recipients of a popular bounty would indeed be an enthusiast. The employer of the carpenter and mason is a builder, and the price of all the material which he purchases is increased by the protective tariff. He receives no bounty which he can divide with his laborers. It would be interesting to find out from the working-men themselves what they think they gain by reason of the taxes imposed upon everything they buy. Is there one of them who supposes that he is benefited by paying to capitalists a bounty of about 40 per cent? What gains the man who carries a hod, or works on the streets, or drives a carriage, or takes care of horses, or writes books, or for the newspapers, or paints pictures, or sets type, or runs a printing press, or drives a locomotive, or is a conductor or a brakeman on a railroad, or practises law, or preaches sermons, or heals bodies, or digs ditches, or belongs in any way to the vast brotherhood of labor that works outside of mills and factories? Can any one of the men who work in this way say how his condition is improved by a law which compels him to pay $29 for a $20 coat; $1.50 for $1.00 worth of sugar; $16.50 for a $10.00 shawl?

How is it with the men who work in mills and factories? Mr. J. E. Thorold Rogers has recently published a book entitled "Six Centuries of Work and Wages." Mr. Rogers is a member of the British Parliament, who has given much study to what we call the labor problem, and he is one of the best and wisest of friends of the working-men of England, a firm believer in the good accomplished through a union of laborers, and a stanch supporter of Mr. Joseph Arch in his work in behalf of the agricultural laborers of Great Britain. Mr. Rogers says this, in speaking of his own country : —

"At present I believe that the workmen of this country, speaking of them in a mass, are better paid than those of any other settled and fully peopled community, if one takes into account not merely the money wages which they earn, but the power which their wages have over commodities."

And the increase of wages has come entirely since the establishment of free trade in England.

Another thing which Mr. Rogers says is worthy of careful thought. It is this : —

"Political economy has indeed taught one lesson of enormous value, though the truth has only been accepted in its fulness among

ourselves. It is that any hindrance put by law or custom in the pur-
chaser's market is a wrong to every one — to the community first, to
the laborer next, to the capitalist employer last. It is due to the facts
that the injury comes last to the capitalist, and that before the mis-
chief is worked out such a person is able to gain abnormal profits by
the losses of others; and that they who get those profits are an organi-
zation; the consumers and the laborers, as a rule, are only a mob; that
protectionist laws, as they are called, exist for a day."

Unless the operatives in mills are benefited by a protective tariff no class of working-men can be helped. Even a
protectionist will admit the soundness of this position. But
to start with, as Mr. Rogers shows, the experience of Great
Britain is that the condition of the working-men was bettered
by the abandonment of protection. What might have been
expected has naturally followed. As soon as the government ceased taxing the earner of wages in the interest of
the earner of interest the former's condition was improved.

Robert Giffen, LL.D., is president of the London Sta-
tistic Society, which was organized for the purpose of ob-
taining information concerning the progress of the working-
classes. In his inaugural address, delivered last November,
Dr. Giffen shows that in the last fifty years the wages of
British operatives have increased wonderfully. For example:
the wages of weavers have increased 150 per cent; of children who are employed in spinning, 160 per cent; of pattern
weavers, 55 per cent. Dr. Giffen thinks that the figures
do not fully indicate the increase that has actually occurred.
At the same time, while the wages of operatives have grown
greater, the wages of seamen have increased from 25 to 69
per cent. The wages of agricultural laborers have also
increased about 60 per cent, while the increase in wages in
Ireland has been very marked.

At the same time the hours of labor have been diminished
very nearly 20 per cent, so that the workman gets from 50
to 100 per cent more money for 20 per cent less work. At

the same time, the price of the· necessaries of life has decreased. Although meat and house-rent are dearer — the latter largely because there has been much improvement in the dwelling-houses of the British workmen — the aggregate of price has diminished, largely owing to the cheapness of wheat. The improvement in the condition of the British workman has been so great that the death rate has decreased; pauperism has diminished ; savings have wonderfully increased, and the schools have multiplied.

Dr. Giffen states the method by which nature works, under a system of taxation such as the revenue reformers propose, so well, that it will be best to quote exactly what he says. He shows that nature, and not a protective tariff, distributes the rewards of toil. He says : —

"It has been shown directly, I believe, that, while the individual incomes of the working-classes have largely increased, the prices of their main articles of consumption have rather declined; and the inference as to their being much better off, which would be drawn from these facts, is fully supported by statistics showing a decline in the rate of mortality, an increase of the consumption of articles in general use, an improvement in general education, a diminution of crime and pauperism, a vast increase of the number of depositors in savings banks, and other evidences of general well-being. Finally, the increase of the return to capital has not been in any way in proportion, the yield in the same amount of capital being less than it was, and the capital itself being more diffused, while the remuneration of labor has enormously increased. The facts are what we should have expected from the conditions of production in recent years. Inventions having been multiplied, and production having been increasingly efficient, while capital has been accumulated rapidly, it is the wages-receivers who must have the benefit. The competition of capital keeps profits down to the lowest point, and workmen consequently get for themselves nearly the whole product of the aggregate industry of the country. It is interesting, nevertheless, to find the facts correspond with what theory should lead us to anticipate."

According to statistics furnished by our own State Department, the wages of Great Britain are much higher than

wages in the continental countries where there are protective tariffs. For example: in England, bricklayers
received $8.16 a week; in Italy, they are paid $4.00; in
Spain, $5.25; in Germany, $4.00; in France, $5.00; in
Belgium, $6.00. This sufficiently illustrates the difference
between these countries.

Mr. Jacob Schoenhof, a New York manufacturer, made a
statement, last winter, before the Ways and Means Committee of the House of Representatives. He showed that
in the cotton factories of this country wages were about
15 per cent higher than in England, but this was made
up by the longer hours of labor, and by the greater skill
of the American operative. The wages in England, however, are 50 per cent higher than those in Germany, and
30 per cent above those of France, while the hours are 56 a
week, against 66 and 72 in this country. In the woollen
industries England pays 50 per cent more wages than Germany, and from 20 to 35 per cent more than France.

In almost every respect, the cost of living in this country
is higher than in Great Britain. House-rent and board are
higher, but some food supplies are cheaper. This is because
much of the food of Great Britain is imported from this
country, and therefore the low prices are the result of foreign competition, and must always exist, because of the
wealth of our agricultural resources. If duties were lowered,
and even if the protective feature of our tariff should be
entirely abandoned, there would be no change in this respect, except to equalize prices, so that the farmer and his
laborers, and the mechanics and operatives of towns and
cities, would secure more for their earnings than they do
now under protection, which means an artificial distribution
of wealth.

Working-men should not be deceived by comparisons made
between the working-men of one city in England and of

another in Massachusetts, — Manchester and Lowell for example. It is not ingenuous to argue, as has been argued, that because there are more savings deposited in the banks of Lowell than of Manchester, therefore the operatives of Lowell can lay aside more from their earnings than operatives similarly employed in Great Britain. The people of two cities may differ in many respects, even of two cities in one of our own States. Between Lowell and Fall River, both in the State of Massachusetts, for example, the statistics of that commonwealth show a great difference. The people of Lowell are thrifty, self-respecting, and saving, while those of Fall River are less so, according to the reports of the Massachusetts Bureau of Labor. When to the ordinary temptations of an undue proportion of drinking-shops, of ill-ventilated, unwholesome dwelling-houses, is added dear land, which precludes the possibility of a working-man saving enough to buy a house for himself and his family, it may easily be seen why the same man may change his nature if he shall be transplanted from one place to the other. An operative who may in Manchester waste the average time in drunkenness, which, according to trustworthy reports, is two days in a week, may, in the different atmosphere of Lowell, become a saver of money. In the one place, it is the thing to get drunk; in the other, it is the thing to have an account in the savings bank.

If capitalists engaged in carrying on protected manufactures are so much interested in keeping up the wages of labor, why do they import cheap labor from abroad? It is a custom in New England and in other parts of the country where the business of manufacturing is carried on, to import labor from Europe and elsewhere because it is cheaper than American labor. Only a year ago a foreign government had occasion to make strong representations to our State Department, because of the conduct of some mill-owners in New Hampshire towards Subjects of Sweden. These Swedes had been brought here at the expense of the mill-owners, and had been supplied with household furniture and provisions from a store connected with the mill. The operatives received small wages, and when they were in debt to the company they were in its power. When there was danger that their earnings would pay their debts, the mill would stop running, and the debts would be given a chance to grow. In this way the Swedes were kept in slavery. When better employment and higher wages were offered them in the neighboring State of Massachusetts, and they attempted to take advantage of the opportunity to better their lot, they were arrested on the ground that they were about to quit the State of New Hampshire for the purpose of defrauding their creditors.

This is not a unique case. The manufacturers, protected or not, seek to secure their working-men for low wages, because low wages is one of the elements that go to the making of large profits. Protectionists say that they desire a high tariff in order that the difference between the high wages of this country and the low wages paid by their foreign competitors may be made up. But as a matter of fact they receive much more than that. At least they do not begin to pay to their laborers what they receive from the taxpayers in the way of bounty, and in very many instances the manufacturer receives in bounty more than the whole cost of his wages.

Speaker Carlisle figures out, from returns of the census of 1880, that it requires two tons of ore to make one ton of pig iron, and that the cost of labor in this quantity of ore is $2.70, and in making pig iron is $3.35 a ton. It takes 1.3 tons of pig iron to make one ton of bar iron, the total cost of labor in the pig being $4.35. According to the testimony of persons engaged in the business, the cost of labor in making one ton of merchant bar iron was, in 1880, $13. Mr. Carlisle, therefore, formulated this statement: —

Cost of labor in	2 tons iron ore	. . . .	$2.70
"	" 1 ton pig iron	. . . .	4.35
"	" 1 ton bar iron	. . . .	13.00
	Total cost of labor	. . . .	$20.05

But the duty on merchant bar iron was $33.60 per ton, " or $13.55 more than enough to pay for all the labor in its production from the time the crude material leaves the earth until it is sent from the mill as a finished article. And besides this," said Mr. Carlisle, in his speech of March 28 and 29, 1882, " there is a duty of 20 per cent on the ore equal to $1.10 per two tons, and a duty of $7 per ton on the pig, making the aggregate duty upon all these forms of product $43.80."

A very interesting and important table was prepared by the Hon. Thomas J. Wood, of Indiana, and used by him in the debate on the Morrison tariff bill. This table showed that the value of the product of all mechanical and manufacturing industries in the census year was $5,369,579,191. The amount paid for labor in the production of this value was $947,953,795. The percentage of value paid for labor was 17.7 ; but the manufacturers received from the taxpayers a bounty of 40 per cent, so that there was an excess of tariff over the cost of labor of 22.3 per cent. Mr. Wood's table will be found in full in the Appendix, but a few extracts showing the excess of bounty over the entire cost of labor will illustrate the important fact that the taxpayers of this country pay to the protected manufactures all the wages, interest, and insurance that they are obliged to expend. The following list shows the excesses of tariff duties over cost of labor : —

```
Agricultural implements . . . . . . . . 12.6 p. c.
Bags, other than paper . . . . . . . . 32.0 "
Leather belting and hose . . . . . . . . 20.7 "
Linen      "        "   . . . . . . . . 20.1 "
Rubber     "        "   . . . . . . . . 17.9 "
Rag carpets . . . . . . . . . . . . . 17.9 "
Carpets, other than rag . . . . . . . . 28.28 "
Clothing, men's,
        cotton . . . . . . . . . . . 13.1 "
        woollen . . . . . . . . . . . 38.1 "
        linen . . . . . . . . . . . 18.1 "
        silk . . . . . . . . . . . 28.1 "
    women's, same.
Cotton goods . . . . . . . . . . . . . 16.7 "
        thread . . . . . . . . . . . 28.6 "
Cotton ties . . . . . . . . . . . . . 20.5 "
Drugs and chemicals . . . . . . . . . 26.2 "
Food preparations . . . . . . . . . . 7.2 "
Fruit-jar trimmings . . . . . . . . 8.5 and 23.5 "
Furnishing goods. Silk . . . . . . . . 27 "
                  Woollen . . . . . . 37 "
                  Linen . . . . . . . 17 "
                  Cotton . . . . . . . 12 "
                  India rubber . . . . . 7 "
Furniture, manufactured . . . . . . . . 5 "
        silk reps . . . . . . . . . . 20 "
        woollen reps . . . . . . . . 25 "
        marble slabs . . . . . . . . 25 "
        haircloths . . . . . . . . . 7 "
        varnish . . . . . . . . . . 10 "
Glass, common window . . . . . . . . 25.1 "
        polished window . . . . . . . 18.0 "
        fluted, or rough plate . . . . . . 7.0 "
        plate glass . . . . . . . . . 42.6 "
        silvered glass . . . . . . . . 14.4 "
        cut, stained, and ornamented . . . . 17.1 "
Hand-knit goods, woollens . . . . . . . 24.1 "
                 cottons . . . . . . . 9.1 "
House-furnishing goods,
        Earthenware, common . . . . 8.7 "
        China, unornamented . . . . . 38.7 "
```

House-furnishing goods — *continued.*

China, ornamented	43.7 p. c.
Cutlery	28.7 "
Glassware	28.7 "
Willowware	13.7 "
Woodenware	18.7 "
Linens	23.7 "
Cottons	18.7 "
Metals	28.7 "
Iron and steel	22.2 "
Iron bolts, nuts, washers, and rivets	25.3 "
Iron doors and shutters	24.1 "
Iron forgings	24.5 "
Iron nails and spikes, cut and wrought	9.4 and 49.9 "
Iron pipe, wrought	28.5 "
Leather	from 4.1 to 35.8 "
Linen goods	19.4 "
Liquors	from 9.2 to 79.59 "
Lumber	average about 16 "
Marble	from 13.4 to 58.1 "
Woollen hats	48.5 "
Woollen goods	49.5 "
Worsted goods	33.3 "

These facts show that the manufacturers receive too much protection if they desire only to make up the difference between wages in this country and wages abroad. They show that the taxpayers bestow upon many of them all the wages that their labor costs them, and from 8 to 50 per cent in addition. That certainly should be a profitable business which costs the owner nothing for labor, interest, or insurance.

What do these unprotected manufacturers do? It has already been stated that they import foreign labor to compete with American working-men, and keep them in slavery at that. Moreover, the testimony of Consul Shaw at Manchester is, that many operatives in British cotton mills are better paid than the men doing the same work in American mills. The reports of the Massachusetts Bureau of Labor

Statistics show a deplorable state of affairs, — small pay,
all the earnings of the operatives eaten up by the mill
stores, unwholesome dwellings, and overworked women
and children. A cigarmaker testifies that in Pennsylvania
the wages earned by men of his craft average from $2 to
$6 a week, lower than the wages paid to Chinese laborers
on the Pacific coast. Mr. John Jarrett testifies that the
condition of the coal miners of Pennsylvania is miserable
and pitiable. They take their lives in their hands, and yet
they are paid a pittance, and their protected employers
make them pay for what they buy 100 per cent more than
other people pay.

The protectionists have a good deal to say about the evil
of employing women and children in factories, and they profess that the benefits which they receive from a high tariff
enable them to remedy this evil. With more than all their
pay-roll provided by the taxpayers of the country, they
ought be able to accomplish this good ; but do they? Statistics show that they are as eager to obtain low-priced labor
as their competitors in Europe. In cotton mills of this
country there are employed girls as young as 7 or 8 years. In
the potteries of Trenton we may find even children of 9
years old at work. As a rule, the women who work in the
great mills of Pennsylvania labor from 7 in the morning
until 6 in the evening, with an hour's intermission, and
for this they receive from $5 to $7 a week. The mills of
Philadelphia employ large numbers of women, and it is the
common practice of these women to lock their children in
the street while the mothers go to work at the factory.
Recently, nurseries have been established where the children
of factory hands can be left at a fixed charge by the day
while their mothers are at work.

The picture that is presented by the honest reports that
are made on labor in factories is not such as that which is

presented by the protectionists in their newspapers and their speeches in Congress. Labor suffers all the exactions that employers can make upon it; and in addition to the grinding force of competition, there must be added all the taxation which a protective tariff imposes upon every consumer, whether he is a merchant, a professional man, a laborer, or even a bounty-fed manufacturer.

The Massachusetts Report of the Statistics of Labor for 1882 shows some remarkable facts. Between 1878 and 1881 the wages of unprotected agriculture increased 14.1 per cent; of blacksmithing, 11.8 per cent; of builders' trades, 4.9 per cent; of printing, 10.2 per cent. But the wages of protected boot and shoemakers decreased 4.4 per cent; of carpet makers, 7.9 per cent. The wages of laborers in protected cotton mills increased 9.1 per cent; in glass factories, 11.6 per cent; hosiery, 13.5 per cent; machines and machinery, 22 per cent. The average increase of all industries was 6.9 per cent.

At the same time groceries advanced 9.1 per cent; provisions, 20.1 per cent; fuel, 30.1 per cent; dry goods, 9 per cent; boots fell in price 1.6 per cent; rents advanced 35.1 per cent; board, 13.7 per cent.

Mr. Wright says, "On all these items entering into the cost of living, the average increase was 21.2 per cent."

Considering all this, does the working-man think that protection is of any benefit to him? In the first place he is taxed heavily on everything which he buys. Most of the working-men of the country receive no return whatever for this increased taxation. They labor in occupations which obtain no share of the vast sum of money taken from the taxpayers for the support of the manufacturers. The wages of those who do work for manufacturers, which are increased by protection, are not increased so much as is the cost of living. Notwithstanding the fact that the protectionists assert that they ask for high duties in order to maintain high wages, they reap the benefit of protection themselves. If they should submit to an average reduction of between 17 and 18 per cent, they would still receive from the tax-payers a bounty large enough not only to pay the difference between wages here and wages in Great Britain, but absolutely all the wages they pay; at the same time this reduction to which they refuse to consent would make wages mean more to the working-men, for the purchasing power of each dollar would be greater. The charitable intentions of the protectionists towards the working-men are not borne out by the story of labor in this country. There are, indeed, model manufacturing towns where the operatives of mills are cared for. They have good homes, good schools, libraries, and many advantages. But the coal miners of Pennsylvania, earning less than a dollar a day, and bled by the truck system; the workers in furnaces, whose wages have been cut down 20 per cent, while their employers have suffered no decrease in the bounty which the taxpayers are compelled to give them; the women of Philadelphia, earning $5 a week for ten hours' daily toil, and leaving their children at the neighbors' or at nurseries, at a cost which must be paid from their scanty earnings, or, if the mothers cannot afford that charge, locking the children in the streets; the strikes which last for months, and which rarely attain their ends; the closing of mills made necessary by over-production; the importation of cheap foreign labor, — all these tell a story which contradicts with its terrible facts the pretended philanthropy of the protectionists.*

* In the census year the average income of hands employed in manufacturing, mechanical, and mining pursuits was $346. Since then, according to the testimony of an expert friendly to the employers, wages have been reduced 20 per cent, so that the average income is now $277.

One of the great evils of the system is that it increases the distance between the poor and the rich. If a manufacturer pays 15 per cent of the cost of production for labor, and receives a protection of 45 per cent, the government is helping him on the road to wealth, while it does not help his working-men to the extent of a solitary cent. The rich are helped in the increase of their riches, and the poor remain where they are. Wealth is distributed not only unequally, but artificially, and the working-man suffers while the protected manufacturer gains. Every vote cast by a laboring man for a protectionist for Congress is a vote against his own interests.

VI.

WHAT PROTECTION DOES FOR TRADE AND COMMERCE.

PROTECTION tends to destroy foreign commerce, and it restricts domestic trade. If it does not accomplish this it fails of its end. The professed purpose of those who advocate a continuance of a high tariff is the prevention of importations, in order that our people may manufacture for themselves all that is necessary for their use. The logical conclusion from this position is that a perfect tariff would prohibit importations of all manufactured articles. The cost to the consumer is a matter of indifference. Protection seeks to compel every American to wear American goods, no matter how badly they may be made or how expensive they may be.

A protectionist looks upon commerce as hostile to the best interests of the country. A hundred years ago the theory that commerce is an object of suspicion was fashionable everywhere except in Holland, and the shrewd Dutchmen profited by the intellectual blindness of their European neighbors. To-day the old fallacy is fashionable again in the United States, and in some countries on the continent of Europe, while Great Britain wisely reaps the rewards of extended commerce.

The manufacturers of this country do not want competition. This does not mean in every instance that they are still unable to compete. In some branches of manufactures they make the best goods that are produced. There is no reason, for example, why cotton goods should be protected. The cotton is grown at our doors, whereas the English mills are obliged to import it from us, paying freight on all that they receive. Then, when their goods are made, they are compelled to pay freight back if they send them to this country. Moreover our machinery is much better than the English machinery. Is not cheaper raw material and freight money over and back across the Atlantic sufficient protection? It would be, but if protection were removed the American cotton manufacturers would have to be content with a larger market and smaller prices. Now we shall see the result of this on the cotton goods trade of the country which produces most of the raw cotton of the world. In 1881 it was estimated by the State Department that the United States produced four fifths of all the cotton of the world; and yet the value of the cotton manufactures in Great Britain was $561,170,000, while that of the manufacturers of this country was less than half as much, $233,-280,000. Taking the figures of a pamphlet published by the State Department, while Mr. Blaine was Secretary of State, we find that the commerce of this country with the world, in cotton goods, was in a shameful condition.

Of all the cotton goods imported into the continent of Africa, and the value reached $25,866,000, $16,049,000 were taken from the United Kingdom, and only $817,000 from the United States.

If this country ought to have any commerce it is certainly with the countries of our own continent, and yet even here our Chinese wall policy of protection keeps us from competing with Great Britain. In 1880 Great Britain exported to Mexico 35,008,200 yards of cotton goods, valued at $2,406,* 000. In the same year the exports of this country to our nearest southern neighbor amounted to only 9,210,398 yards, valued at $832,235. Although our manufacturers are thousands of miles nearer the Mexican market than the British manufacturers are, our plain cottons cost 6.97 cents a yard while the British sold at 6.06 cents, and our prints cost 7.84 cents, and the British prints 7.22 cents.

The showing as to the Central American trade is still worse. In 1880 the United Kingdom exported to Central America cotton goods to the value of $2,161,000, while the exports of this country amounted to only $77,736.

Great Britain exported to the West Indies $9,582,000 worth of cotton goods. The French exports amounted to $1,221,000, while those of the United States reached only the insignificant sum of $956,802.

The prices per yard of the goods of the two countries are significant. They were as follows : —

Prices of goods exported to Central America.

	Plain. cts.	Prints. cts.
From Great Britain	5.23	7.15
" United States	6.89	7.14

And yet with this small difference in favor of the American manufacturer in the price of prints, the Central American market took $855,000 worth of prints from Great Britain and only $28,322 worth from the United States. The reason is plain. Great Britain's policy is to seek a foreign market, and her manufacturers, therefore, make goods that satisfy the demand.

The prices in the West Indies were as follows : —

	Plain. cts.	Prints. cts.
Great Britain	6.72	7.28
United States	8.68	10.63

The following table shows the export of cotton goods to the principal South American countries : —

	Values.	
	Great Britain.	United States.
Colombia	$3,163,000	$586,692
Venezuela	1,449,000	140,316
Brazil	17,182,000	687,523
Uruguay	3,081,000	52,524
Argentine Republic	4,816,000	133,647
Chili	5,162,000	217,869

The value of the cottons sent from England to British India in 1880 was $102,870,000, while the value of American cottons sent there was $136,043.

Great Britain sent to China and Hong Kong cottons valued at $29,774,000, and the United States sent $373,568.

Japan received $9,784,000 worth of British goods, and $33,331 worth of American.

The trade of the two countries with Europe is shown as follows : —

	Great Britain.	United States.
Denmark	$1,871,000	$2,812
Germany	14,648,000	166,029*
Holland	12,525,000	3,847
Belgium	5,273,000	12,531
France	8,615,000	21,507
Spain	2,231,000	none
Portugal	4,150,000	1,200
Italy	7,064,000	10,566
Austria-Hungary	936,000	2,650

* The prices of American goods were cheaper than those of British. The American goods cost 7.4 cents a yard for plain, and 9.09 cents for print. The British goods cost 8.14 and 9.22 cents.

The protectionists of the United States deliberately close the door on this important commerce, because they prefer to receive the high price of the home market to competing with the manufacturers of Great Britain, who pay more for their raw cotton, operate with not so good machinery, and who yet study the demands of the world, supply all the markets of the world, and who derive from lower prices a greater prosperity than our own manufacturers can boast. The reports of our consuls show that American cottons are better than British, and when they do enter into competition are often sold cheaper than the British cottons. But the foreign demand is only supplied by Americans when our own market is glutted. Whenever there is a large home demand our manufacturers turn their backs on the foreigners and reap for a time the high prices at home which the bounty enables them to charge. Instability is the general result of the protective system, — abnormal profits one day, and gloomy depression the next; four months running day and night, another four months of half-time, and another of strikes, lock-outs, or entire shutting down; the sale of goods at unreasonably high prices, or their exportation at rates which cannot pay.

There are not enough cotton goods manufactured by power looms to supply the wear of the world. According to our State Department, it is estimated that the Chinese alone wear out 7,300,000,000 yards of cottons annually, made on hand looms. Why not supply the enormous demand of a people whose chief clothing is of cotton, and who are at the other end of the route of the Pacific Mail Steamship Company?

The United States can compete and compete successfully with Great Britain. The difference between the cotton trade statistics of Canada and those of Mexico are very suggestive. For some reason, our manufacturers have

found it to their profit to cultivate the trade of Canada, and
the result is that they exported to that country, in 1880,
cotton goods to the value of $2,766,779, while Great Brit-
ain's exports were valued at $3,771,165, and the exports of
plain goods were three times as many as those of Great
Britain. The prices per yard were as follows: —

	Plain. cts.	Print. cts.
Great Britain	6.75	8.25
United States	6.75	7

The story of our cotton goods trade is the story of all
our commerce. Contrast the export trade of Great Britain and the United States for 1881, with the following
countries: —

	Great Britain.	United States.
Africa	$68,754,000	$4,581,924
Canada	43,583,808	36,704,112
Mexico	6,235,000	11,191,000
Central America . . .	3,310,000	1,626,000
Colombia	5,220,000	5,383,000
Venezuela	2,123,000	2,770,000
British Guiana	4,200,C00	1,723,000
Dutch Guiana	260,000	289,000
Brazil	33,607,000	9,200,000
Uruguay	6,877,000	1,612,000
Argentine Republic . . .	12,103,000	3,121,000
Chili	12,219,000	1,520,000
Peru	1,847,000	94,000

Of the exports of leading manufactured articles exported
to South America, Great Britain's exports amount to
$79,258,000, the exports of France to $58,113,000, and
those of the United States to $25,220,000. Great Britain,
in 1880, exported to the several countries of Europe goods
of the value of $617,576,000. The exports of France
amounted to $625,963,000, and those of the United States
to $765,701,000. Of these exports Great Britain exported
only $389,132,000 of British goods, France $479,819,000 of

French goods, while the United States exported $754,995,-
000 of American goods. But this great exportation was
made up chiefly of the products of the soil. As has been
shown before, it is the farmer who must stand the competition of the foreign market. In the fiscal year 1881, the
total exports of this country amounted to $883,915,947. Of
this amount, $748,536,043 was the value of the natural
products, and $135,379,904 of manufactured articles. And
these were the principal items of the natural products : —

Bread and Breadstuffs	$268,890,139
Cotton	247,696,746
Provisions	151,428,268
	$668,015,153

Our commerce, then, is at the best not much different
than it would have been had the government never taxed
the farmer and the laborer to maintain the manufacturer.
It is a commerce in which we exchange the products of the
soil for the manufactured articles of other countries. We
do not even make enough cotton goods for ourselves. In
1881 we imported $234,962,511 of manufactured articles,
and $31,219,361 of this was the value of foreign cotton
goods brought into the country, while the cottons we sent
abroad were valued at only $13,571,287.

Protection has not only failed to give the country the
home market which it promised, but it has also failed to
give us the diversified interests for which we pay in tariff
taxes, and bounties. It does not even give us enough high-
priced American fabrics, and it obstructs and has destroyed
our foreign commerce. The shipping trade is ruined. In
1880 this country imported goods from Europe amounting
to $340,831,000, and only $11,863,000 came in American
vessels; of the $754,995,000 exports, of the same year, only
$46,707,000 went in American vessels.

In 1855 there were built in this country for the foreign
carrying trade 400 vessels. In 1879 only 35 were built.
On the other hand, the tonnage of Great Britain engaged
in the carrying trade with this country has increased, since
1857, from 950,000 tons to nearly 6,000,000 tons. In 1857,
this country had more than 4,000,000 tons engaged in the
foreign trade; now it has hardly 600,000 tons. Last year
we paid $120,000,000 freight money to foreign shipowners.

The protective tariff prevents trading with foreign countries; it throws obstacles in the way of American citizens
who desire to engage in the business of importing goods;
it has destroyed the carrying trade; it prevents the citizens
of this country from earning the $120,000,000 of freight
money annually paid to foreign ships. During the last year
the flag of the United States was not once seen in the Suez
Canal, and it is rarely found in ports where it was once the
best known ensign of the world. Can the commerce of the
country afford any longer to cripple its resources and limit
its field, for the sake of increasing the profits of the protected manufacturers?

VII.

WHAT A LOW TARIFF DID FOR THE COUNTRY.

BETWEEN 1846 and 1860 the country had a low tariff.
Under the law of 1846 the average rate of duty was about
25 per cent, and under the act of 1857 it was about 20 per
cent. There never was a period of greater prosperity in the
history of the country.

In 1850 the cash value of farms was $3,271,575,426, and
in 1860 it was $6,645,045,057, an increase of 103 per cent.

In 1870 the value of farms was $9,262,853,861 in currency, an increase of only 39 per cent over the gold valuation of 1860. In 1880 the value of farms was $10,197,096,766, an increase of a little more than 10 per cent over the value of 1870. From 1850 to 1860 the value of farming implements increased 63.50 per cent. In the next decade the increase was only 36 per cent in currency, while from 1870 to 1880 the increase was only 20.66 per cent.

From 1830 to 1840 the aggregate value of all real and personal property increased 40 per cent ; from 1840 to 1850 37 per cent. In 1850 this aggregate value was $7,135,-780,228; in 1860 it was $16,159,616,068, an increase of 126 per cent. In 1870 the aggregate value was $30,068,518,507, in currency, being an apparent increase of a little more than 85 per cent. In 1860 the total State and local taxation was $94,186,746, but in 1870 it had reached the enormous sum of $280,591,521, an increase of 198 per cent, although the value of property had increased only 85 per cent. An examination of the report of the Superintendent of the Census for 1870 shows that the increase in the value of real and personal property from 1850 to 1860 was more than 184 per cent, instead of 126 per cent, and that instead of an increase of 85 per cent from 1860 to 1870, there was an actual decrease of more than 3 per cent. This arises from what the superintendent says was an undervaluation of property in 1860, by carelessness, of from 20 to 30 per cent, while the nominal valuation of property was increased in 1870 from 30 to 40 per cent through the effects of currency inflation and other causes. Making the necessary allowances for these sums, we have $20,199,520,085 as the proper valuation for 1860, and $19,544,537,030 as the true valuation for 1870. If our wealth had increased from 1860 to 1880 at the same rate as it did from 1850 to 1860, it would have reached, in 1880, $83,000,000,000 instead of $43,300,000,000.

There was the same wonderful increase in our manufacturing and mechanical industries. In 1850 the total value of the products of mechanical and manufacturing industries was $1,019,106,616; in 1860 it was $1,885,861,676, an increase of 87 per cent, although the population of the country had increased only 35.50 per cent. From 1860 to 1870 the actual increase was only 52 per cent.

The increase in the production of coal, which, according to the protection leaders, indicates better than any other single branch of industry the progress of all manufacturing enterprises, was very wonderful between 1850 and 1860. The following table shows this increase: —

	per cent.
Gain in number of mines	22.30
" " value of yearly products	182
" " " " material used	1017
" " amount paid as wages	137
" " number of hands employed	143.33
" " amount of capital invested	253

In Pennsylvania the capital invested in the production of coal was 331 per cent greater in 1860 than in 1850, and the value of the coal produced increased 179.90 per cent. In Maryland the increase was nearly 137 per cent; in Ohio nearly 127 per cent; in Indiana nearly 652 per cent; in Illinois it was 1708 per cent; in Iowa it was 2204 per cent; in Kentucky it was 200 per cent; and in Alabama nearly 237 per cent.

During the fiscal year 1860 our foreign trade amounted to $687,372,176, which was $45,000,000 greater than ever before. We built 2,265 ships and barques, between 1850 and 1860, and only 860 during the next decade, and only 608 between 1870 and 1880. Then our tonnage engaged in all trades, coasting as well as foreign, was 5,353,868 tons; now, after the expiration of twenty years, it is 4,068,035 tons.

The social and intellectual condition of the people kept pace with the material progress. Schools, churches, and libraries flourished. The product of the printing establishments of the United States increased 107.60 per cent from 1860 to 1870, while the capital invested increased during the same time, 143 per cent. Wonderful as this is, it does not tell the story of the prosperity and growth of the preceding decade under a revenue tariff. Then the products of the printing houses increased 168 per cent, while the capital invested increased 235 per cent. In New England the increased product was more than 96 per cent, and in the Middle States 139 per cent. Pennsylvania increased her product 250 per cent, and New Jersey 322 per cent.

In the eleven western States and Territories, the increase was 572 per cent. The State of New York increased 104.60 per cent, and actually turned out in 1860 more than the whole country produced in 1850.

In 1850 we had 18,417 postoffices and 178,672 miles of post routes, but in 1860 we had 28,498 post-offices and 245,-594 miles of post routes, an increase of 55 per cent in the number of offices, and 35 per cent in miles of roads. In 1880, 20 years later, we had 42,989 postoffices, being an increase of only 50 per cent over the number in 1860, and 343,-888 miles of post roads, being an increase of 42.50 per cent since 1860.

In the manufacture of paper the United States increased the value of its product 106.50 per cent from 1860 to 1870, while the capital invested increased 126.50 per cent, but from 1850 to 1860 the value of the product increased more than 108 per cent, and the capital invested increased nearly 180 per cent. The increase in the number of hands employed was 73.50 per cent, and in the total amount of wages paid 89 per cent. Pennsylvania alone increased her product 128 per cent.

Up to the end of the year 1850 we had constructed only
9,021 miles of railroad in this country, but at the close of
1860, we had 30,635 miles, being an increase of 239.50 per
cent in ten years. At the close of the year 1870 we had 52,-
914 miles of railroad, being an increase of only a little more
than 72 per cent over the number in 1860, notwithstanding
the government had since 1860 granted millions of acres of
public lands, and issued its bonds to the amount of millions
of dollars to various railroad companies to aid in the con-
struction of their lines. In 1880 we had 88,237 miles of
railroad, an increase of 66.66 per cent during the decade.

The value of the output of our woollen mills from 1850 to
1860 increased nearly 42.50 per cent, while from 1870 to 1880
it increased only 22.57 per cent. The number of hands employed increased 18.50 per cent, and the total wages increased
36.80 per cent. In New England the product of the woollen
mills increased 62 per cent; the increase in Rhode Island being 176 per cent; Massachusetts, 53.70 per cent; New Jersey,
21.57 per cent; Vermont, 61.39 per cent; and Maine, 83.46
per cent.

The value of the carpet manufactures increased 45.40 per
cent. The increase in the number of hands employed was
8 per cent, and the increase in the total of wages paid was
nearly 24 per cent. The compensation received by each
hand was 15 per cent more in 1860 than in 1850. In the
Middle States the value of the product increased 80.90 per
cent; in Ohio, 208 per cent; in Maine, 47.30 per cent; in
Massachusetts, 44.80 per cent; in New York, 32.90 per cent;
and in Pennsylvania 138 per cent.

The products of the manufactures of hosiery increased
608 per cent. The Eastern States increased 481 per cent;
the Middle States, 695.50 per cent; and the Western States,
445 per cent. Pennsylvania increased 276 per cent; Connecticut, 523 per cent; New Jersey, 379 per cent; Massachu-

setts, 373 per cent; Maryland, 255 per cent; Ohio, 278 per cent; and Missouri, 726 per cent.

The production of iron ore increased 79.20 per cent, while the capital invested increased 126.30 per cent. The total number of hands employed in this industry was 45 per cent greater in 1860 than in 1850, and the total amount of wages paid was nearly 57 per cent greater.

The production of pig iron increased 54 per cent in the United States. In the State of Pennsylvania it increased 82 per cent; in New Jersey, 105 per cent; in Kentucky, 27 per cent; and in New York, 53 per cent. At the same time the price of pig iron was reduced from $23.43 in 1850 to $21.13 in 1860.

The increase in the value of bar, sheet, and railroad iron was more than 100 per cent. The number of hands employed increased 66 per cent, and the amount of wages paid 80 per cent. In this industry Pennsylvania increased her production 106 per cent; Delaware, 230 per cent; Maryland, 104 per cent; Ohio, 173 per cent; Kentucky, 68 per cent; and Virginia, 104 per cent.

Iron castings increased in value of the product 74.80 per cent. In the Middle States the value of the product was more than 100 per cent greater in 1860 than in 1850; in Pennsylvania, 100 per cent; and in Maine more than 520 per cent.

In the production of hardware there was an increase of 56.70 per cent, while the capital invested increased 90 per cent, and the number of hands employed increased 52.50 per cent. The New England States increased 100 per cent, and made more hardware in 1860 than all the States made in 1850. Connecticut alone increased her production 103.80 per cent; and New Jersey, 360 per cent. The Western States increased their product 74 per cent, while the State of Ohio increased 99 per cent.

The steel industry had its birth during the decade from 1850 to 1860. The product increased 99.50 per cent, while the capital invested increased over 3,000 per cent, the hands employed 1,770 per cent, and the wages paid 123.60 per cent.

In the manufacture of machinery, steam engines, etc., including locomotives, hay and cotton presses, and cotton and woollen machinery, the value of the product increased 66.60 per cent in the whole country, but in the Western States the increase was 217 per cent.

The manufacture of sewing machines was scarcely known in 1850, but in 1860 the value of the product was $4,247,820.

During this prosperous decade, when every branch of commerce flourished, when labor was adequately rewarded, and when the American mechanic was prosperous, when not only the material but the intellectual and moral forces of the country grew rapidly and healthfully, the government effected two loans, amounting in the aggregate to $40,000,-000. One half of this indebtedness consisted of Treasury notes bearing six per cent interest, and redeemable at the expiration of one year from date. These notes were issued under the act of December 23, 1857, and although part of them bore only three per cent interest they were sold at par.

The other loan of $20,000,000 was effected by the sale of bonds, authorized by the act of June 14, 1858. They were made redeemable fifteen years after date, and bore interest at the rate of five per cent per annum. They were sold at a premium of from two to seven per cent in gold. Since that time the government has never sold a bond, no matter what the rate of interest might be, for any such premium as was obtained for the bonds issued under the act of 1858.

An act passed June 22, 1860, was simply a funding act. It authorized the issue of bonds or stocks to an amount not exceeding $21,000,000, bearing interest not exceeding six per cent, and redeemable not more than 20 years after date. The money raised was to be used only in the redemption of Treasury notes previously issued. Under this act there was raised the sum of $7,022,000, the bonds issued bearing interest at the rate of five per cent. Some of these bonds were sold at par, and the remainder at a premium of nearly 1.50 per cent.

No other decade excepting that during which the country was blessed with a revenue tariff has such a story of prosperity to tell as these ten years have stamped on our history. No other decade will have such a story to tell until the government ceases to tax four fifths of the people for the benefit of a small fraction of the other fifth.

Tables contrasting wages paid in Great Britain, Germany, and France.

[Values reduced to American dollars: English shilling and German mark, 24 cents; franc, 19 cents.]

Class of occupation.	Great Britain.			France, 1881.	United States consular reports, 1881.	Germany. Table of statistics of Society "Concordia," 1882.
	Glasgow, 1865.	Manchester and neighborhood, 1880.	East Lancashire, 1880.			
Hours work in week	66.	56.	56.	72.	66 to 72.	66 to 72.
Scutchers:						Reports from 134 factory towns of the empire give the earnings of weavers in power mills at rates varying from $1.50 to $4.50 per week, mostly of 66 hours (some with 72 and 78 hours). The earnings are: 2 at $1.44; 7 at $1.92; 9 at $2.16; 16 at $2.40; 7 at $2.64; 18 at $2.87; 10 at $3.12; 13 at $3.36; 20 at $3.60; 6 at $3.84; 10 at $4.32; 2 at $5.04; average, $3.00 for men; women's earnings, of course, are considerably less.
Men		$5 40				
Girls	$2 06	2 04				
Strippers:						
Men		5 40	$5 28 to $5 76	$4 34		
Lads	2 76	3 50				
Grinders:						
Men	4 68	5 16	5 28 to 5 76	4 34	$2 86 to $3 09	
Lads		3 50				
Lap and can tenders, lads	2 40	2 16				
Drawer frame tenders, women		3 67	3 90 to 4 56	2 84	2 14 to 2 38	
Roving and slubbing, women		3 60	3 90 to 4 56		2 10 to 2 25	
Card winders:						
Men	5 28	5 87		3 47	2 50 to 3 70	
Women		2 88				
Overlookers, men	6 48	9 24	8 40 to 12 00			
Mule spinners, men	6 24	6 90	7 20 to 8 40	5 79	3 57 to 4 52	
Piecers, lads						
Engine driver	5 76 to 9 60		5.04 to 12 00	6 08	4 28 to 8 57	

Machinery.

Occupations.	1865.	England. 1880.—Birmingham.	1880.—Dundee.	1880.—Glasgow.	1880.—Reports of chambers of commerce.	Germany. 1882.—Statistical tables of Concordia.
Hours	66–72	54	54	54		
Pattern-makers .	$7 92	$7 92	$6 96	$7 56	Yearly earnings in foundry and machine shops for men unskilled, $130 to $200. Skilled, from $225 to $300.	Weekly earnings of skilled men in machine shops, 232 towns: 8 at $2.40; 6 at $2.64; 26 at $2.87; 21 at $3.36; 65 at $3.00; 13 at $3.84; 9 at $4.08; 58 at $4.32; 5 at $4.60; κat $4.80; 4 at $5.04; 1 at $5.38; 5 at $5.76; 1 at $6.24; 1 at $6.48; 1 at $6.96. Average for the Empire, $3.82.
Iron-moulders . .	8 64	8 40	7 20	. . .		
Brass-moulders . .	. . .	8 40	6 72	. . .		
Steam-hammermen .	. . .	12 96	. . .	. . .		
Forgemen	. . .	. . .	16 80	. . .		
Smiths	. . .	8 16	6 48	7 32		
Strikers . . . {	3 36 to 4 32	5 04	4 56	5 04		
Planers	. . .	6 72	6 00	6 72		
Turners	7 20	7 68	6 72	6 72		
Fitters	7 20	7 68	6 24	7 14		
Stokers	. . .	4 80	5 14	6 12		
Carpenters . . .	. . .	7 20	6 72	7 03		
Bricklayers . . .	. . .	7 20	. . .	. . .		
Laborers . . . {	3 60 to 4 80	4 32	3 84	4 08		
Boiler-makers . .	8 16	. . .	6 48	7 32		

Boots and Shoes.

Description of occupation.	Great Britain.—Leicester and neighborhood, 1880.	France.	Germany. Tables of Concordia.
Hours	56	In France wages of shoemakers are between five and six francs a day. (Report of Secretary Evarts, State of Labor in Europe, 1878.)	In Germany wages for men in the shoe industry vary from $4, paid in Frankfort (o. M.), Karlsruhe $3.84, to Offenbach (o. M.) $3.00 — the latter the centre of a large manufacturing industry in this line.
Sewing machinists, men	7 20		
Sewing machinists, women	3 80		
Cutters, men . . .	5 04		
Clickers, men . . .	6 48		
Riveters, men . . .	6 00		
Machine operators, men	6 72		
Finishers	7 20		

The following tables were presented to the Statistical Society of Great Britain by its president, Robert Giffen, LL.D., November 20, 1883 :

Comparison of wages fifty years ago and at the present time.

[From miscellaneous statistics of the United Kingdom and Porter's Progress of the Nation.]

Occupation.	Place.	Wages per week.		Increase.	
		Fifty years ago.	Present time.	Amount.	Per cent.
		£ s. d.	£ s. d.	s. d.	
Carpenters	Manchester . .	1 4 0	1 14 0	10 0	42
Carpenters	Glasgow . . .	14 0	1 6 0	12 0	85
Bricklayers	Manchester a .	1 4 0	1 16 0	12 0	50
Bricklayers	Glasgow . . .	15 0	1 7 .0	12 0	80
Masons.	Manchester a .	1 4 0	1 9 10	5 10	24
Masons	Glasgow . . .	14 0	1 3 8	9 8	69
Miners	Staffordshire .	b2 8	b4 0	1 4	50
Pattern-weavers	Huddersfield .	16 0	1 5 0	9 0	55
Wool-scourers	Huddersfield .	17 0	1 2 0	5 0	30
Mule-spinners	Huddersfield .	1 5 6	1 10 0	4 6	20
Weavers	Huddersfield .	12 0	1 6 0	14 0	115
Warpers and beamers . .	Huddersfield .	17 0	1 7 0	10 0	58
Winders and reelers . . .	Huddersfield .	6 0	11 0	5 0	83
Weavers (men)	Bradford . . .	8 3	1 6 0	12 3	150
Reeling and warping . .	Bradford . . .	7 9	15 6	7 9	100
Spinning (children) . . .	Bradford . . .	4 5	11 6	7 1	160

a 1825.   b Wages per day.

Comparison of seamen's money-wages per month, 1850 and the present time.

[From the Progress of Merchant Shipping Returns.]

	1850 — sailing.	Present time — steam.	Increase.	
			Amount.	Per cent.
	£ s. d.	£ s. d.	£ s. d.	
Bristol	2 5 0	3 15 0	1 10 0	66
Glasgow	2 5 0	3 10 0	1 5 0	55
Liverpool (1).	2 10 0	3 7 6	16 6	33
Liverpool (2).	2 10 0	4 5 0	1 15 0	70
Liverpool (3).	2 5 0	3 0 0	15 0	33
Liverpool (4).	2 0 0	2 10 0	10 0	25
Liverpool (5).	2 2 6	3 0 0	17 6	40
London (1)	2 5 0	3 15 0	1 10 0	66
London (2)	2 10 0	3 17 6	1 7 6	55
London (3)	2 5 0	3 5 0	1 0 0	45
London (4)	2 5 0	3 10 0	1 5 0	55
London (5)	2 0 0	3 7 6	1 7 6	69
London (6)	2 0 0	3 7 6	1 7 6	69

Paupers in receipt of relief in the years given below.

	1849.	1881.
England	934,000	803,000
Scotland	a 122,000	102,000
Ireland	620,000	109,000
United Kingdom	1,676,000	1,014,000

a 1859.

Average attendance at schools aided by parliamentary grants.

	1851.	1881.
England	239,000	2,863,000
Scotland	32,000	410,000

Savings.

	1831.	1881.
Number of depositors	429,000	4,140,000
Amount of deposits	£13,719,000	£80,334,000
Amount per depositor	£32	£19

Table showing cost of English and American steel rails, and the effect of duty on prices.

Year.	Price in England, free on board.	English price.	Price of American steel rails in gold.	Difference in price.	Rate of duty.	
					Per cent.	Per ton.
	£ s. d.					
1864	17 12 0	$85 65	$148 50	$62 85	45	
1865	16 7 0	79 56	127 50	47 94	45	
1866	14 10 0	70 56	117 50	46 94	45	
1867	13 10 0	65 70	113 28	47 58	45	
1868	12 12 0	61 32	105 00	43 68	45	
1869	11 6 0	54 99	97 38	42 39	45	
1870	10 7 0	50 37	91 17	40 80	45	
1871	11 6 0	54 99	91 18	36 19	. . .	$28 00
1872	13 18 0	67 04	98 43	30 79	. . .	28 00
1873	16 9 0	80 05	103 91	23 06	. . .	28 00
1874	13 2 0	68 75	85 76	17 01	. . .	28 00
1875	9 2 0	44 28	59 75	14 97	. . .	28 00
1876	6 12 0	32 12	44 97	12 75	. . .	28 00
1877	6 0 0	29 20	42 08	12 88	. . .	28 00
1878	5 5 0	25 55	42 00	16 45	. . .	28 00
1879	5 10 6	26 88	48 25	21 37	. . .	28 00
1880	7 1 6	34 36	67 50	33 14	. . .	28 00
1881	6 10 0	31 53	60 00	28 47	. . .	28 00
1882	6 7 6	31 10	57 00	25 90	. . .	28 00

SCHEDULE. — *Statement showing amount of incidental taxes annually imposed on the people of the United States in the increased cost of home products, by reason of discriminating duties on imported articles of like character, together with the value of such home products, the amount of wages paid, and number of hands employed, and the imports and duties received thereon, for the year 1882.*

Articles affected by the tariff.	Merchandise imported during fiscal year ended June 30, 1882.			Value of home products, census year, 1880.	Average number of hands employed, Boys under 16 and girls under 15 counted as one-half a hand.	Total amount in wages during the year.	Estimated rate of increase ad valorem.	Incidental taxes, being the increased cost of home products by reason of the tariff.
	Values.	Duty received.	Average ad valorem rates.					
			Per cent.				*Per cent.*	
Chemical products	$21,517,169	$6,718,561	31.32	$117,377,324	28,895	$11,840,704	20	$23,475,464
Earthenware and glassware	13,822,043	6,693,257	48.42	31,632,309	30,674	13,130,403	45	14,234,539
Metals — iron, steel, and metal manufactures	74,427,988	30,358,936	40.79	604,553,460	290,000	122,648,191	20	120,910,692
Wood and woodenware	8,654,327	1,589,851	18.37	311,928,884	185,426	47,817,199	15	46,789,332
Sugar and molasses	94,540,269	49,210,573	52.05	(*)	(*)		40	4,846,714
Tobacco, &c.	8,216,132	6,000,961	73.03	118,665,366	81,809	25,041,267	25	29,666,341
Cotton and cotton goods	34,868,044	13,482,167	38.67	210,950,383	170,363	45,614,419	20	42,190,076
Hemp, jute, and flax goods	33,578,076	9,844,652	29.32	5,518,866	4,329	1,238,149	20	1,105,773
Wool and woollens	47,679,502	29,254,234	61.36	267,182,914	145,341	47,351,628	40	106,873,165
Silk and silk goods	38,535,475	22,632,490	58.73	41,003,045	28,554	9,146,705	50	20,516,522
Books, paper, &c.	4,923,620	1,406,787	28.57	65,960,405	25,274	9,895,995	20	13,192,081
Sundries	62,410,690	17,272,269	27.68	665,699,693	337,216	129,881,399	20	133,139,938
Total	433,173,335	194,464,758	. . .	2,440,502,649	1,327,881	463,006,049	. . .	556,938,637

* Planters' products for 1880 were: Sugar, 196,759,200 pounds; molasses, 16,573,273 gallons. Number and wages of laborers not stated.

SCHEDULE. — *Statement showing value of product, amount paid for hired labor, and ratio of latter to value of product, in all industries, as returned at the Tenth Census, with rate of duty (tariff) on each industry or article of chief value entering into the same; also excess of tariff over cost of labor in all protected industries.*

					Per cent.
Average paid for labor					17.7
Average rate of duty, under act March 3, 1883					40.0
Excess of tariff over cost of labor					22.3

Mechanical and manufacturing industries.	Each industry during census year (1880).			(Tariff.) Rate of duty.	Excess of tariff over cost of labor.
	Value of product.	Amount paid for labor.	Percent. paid for labor.		
All industries	5,369,579,191	947,953,795	17.7	40 per cent.	22.3 per cent.
Agricultural implements	68,640,486	15,359,610	22.4	Wood — chief value, 35 p. c.	12.6 p. c.
				Iron or steel — chief value, 45 p. c.	22.6 p. c.
Ammunition	1,904,966	361,778	19.0	Shot, 3c. lb.	43.7 p. c.
				Shell, 45 p. c.	26.0 p. c.
				Gun-wads, 35 p. c.	26.0 p. c.
				Percussion-caps, 40 p. c.	21 p. c.
				Gunpowder — value 20 cents or less per lb., 6c. per lb.; valued over 20 cents per lb., 10c.	
Artificial feathers and flowers	4,879,324	1,081,040	22.0	Crude, 25 p. c.	16.6 p. c.
				Dressed, 50 p. c.	3 p. c.
Artificial limbs	137,024	43,833	32.0	35 p. c.	28 p. c.
Awnings and tents	1,986,942	334,463	17.0	35 p. c.	3 p. c.
Axle grease	365,048	41,407	11.3	10 p. c.	18 p. c.
Babbitt metal and solder	262,950	18,745	7.1	Manufactures of metals, n. o. s., 45 p. c.	—1.3 p. c.
Bagging, flax, hemp, and jute	3,511,653	827,769	23.6	Valued at 7c. or less per sq. yd., 1½c. per lb., valued over 7c. per sq. yd., 2c. per lb.	37.9 p. c.
					7.9 p. q.

Statement showing value of product, amount paid for hired labor, &c. — Continued.

Mechanical and manufacturing industries.	Each industry during census year (1880).			(Tariff.) Rate of duty.	Excess of tariff over cost of labor.
	Value of product.	Amount paid for labor.	Percent. paid for labor.		
Bags:					
Other than paper	$9,726,600	$776,028	8.0	40 p. c.	32.0 p. c.
Paper	4,112,566	439,620	10.7	15 p. c. as manufactures of paper	4.3 p. c.
Baking and yeast powders	4,760,598	466,252	9.8	20 p. c. (n. e.).	10.2 p. c.
Baskets, rattan and willow ware	1,992,851	657,405	33.0	30 p. c.	– 3.0 p. c.
Bellows	26,900	6,875	25.6	Wood and leather, 35 p. c.	9.4 p. c.
Bells	1,065,824	280,169	26.3	Metal, 45 p. c.	19.4 p. c.
Belting and hose:					
Leather	6,525,737	606,087	9.3	45 p. c.	18.7 p. c.
Linen	23,000	4,500	19.6	30 p. c.	20.7 p. c.
Rubber	1,085,000	131,721	12.1	40 p. c.	20.4 p. c.
Billiard tables and materials	2,289,758	400,179	17.5	30 p. c.	17.9 p. c.
Blacking	1,491,474	168,183	11.3	35 p. c.	17.5 p. c.
Blacksmithing	43,774,271	11,126,001	25.4	25 p. c.; Bar-iron, .8, .1, and 1.1c. per lb. Hoop, band, or scroll, 1, 1.2, and 1.4c. per lb. Axles, axle bars or blanks, 2½c. per lb. Hammers and sledges, 2½c. per lb. Bolts, blanks, rivets, 2½c. per lb. Chains, 1½, 2, and 2½c. per lb. Hob horseshoe nails, 4c. per lb. Ox, mule, horseshoes and spikes, 2c. per lb. Steel bars, coils, and sheets, valued at not, over 4c. per lb., 45 p. c.; valued above 4 and not above 7c. per lb., 2c. per lb.; valued above 7 and not above 10c. per lb., 2¾c. per lb.; valued above 10c. per lb, 3½c. per lb. Files, rasps, and floats, 35.75, $1.50 and $2 per doz., according to size. Wire rods, .6c. per lb. Borax, 3c. per lb. The average ad valorem rate of all iron and steel, and manufactures of, is about 40 p. c.	13.7 p. c.

Average, 15 p.c.

				Duty	Average, —3.4 p. c.
Blueing	344,824	50,245	14.6	20 p. c.	5.4 p. c.
Rope, ivory, and lampblack .	661,376	80,249	12.1	25 p. c.	12.9 p. c.
Bookbinding and blank-book making .	11,976,764	3,027,349	32.8	Leather, 30 p. c.; Paper, 15 p. c.; Gold leaf, 30.8 p. c.; Ink, 30 p. c.; Twine, 35 p. c.	Average, —3.4 p. c.
Boot and shoe:					
Cut stock	7,531,635	735,482	9.8	30 p. c.	20.2 p. c.
Findings	2,144,945	451,075	21.0	30 p. c.	9.0 p. c.
Uppers	790,842	170,425	21.5	20 p. c.	—1.5 p. c.
Including custom work and repairing .	196,920,481	60,995,144	25.9	30 p. c.	4.1 p. c.
Rubber	9,705,724	1,469,038	15.1	25 p. c.	9.9 p. c.
Boxes:					
Cigar	2,903,465	748,657	25.8	30 p. c.	4.2 p. c.
Fancy and paper . . .	7,665,553	2,373,948	31.0	35 p. c.	4.0 p. c.
Wooden, packing . . .	12,687,068	2,769,135	21.8	30 p. c.	8.2 p. c.
Brass and copper, rolling .	14,329,731	2,524,169	17.6	45 p. c.	27.4 p. c.
Brass castings . . .	10,804,742	2,729,794	25.3	45 p. c.	19.7 p. c.
Brass ware	1,523,098	411,329	27.0	45 p. c.	18.0 p. c.
Bread and other bakery products	65,824,896	9,411,328	14.3	20 p. c.	5.7 p. e.
Brick and tile . . .	32,833,587	13,443,532	40.9	20 p. c.	—20.9 p. c.
Bridges	8,978,122	1,882,179	21.0	Wood, 35 p. c.; Metal, 45 p. c.	14.0 p. c.; 24.0 p. c.
Bronze castings . . .	670,912	64,072	9.5	45 p. c.	35.5 p. c.
Brooms and brushes . .	10,560,855	2,424,040	23.0	Brooms, 25 p. c.; Brushes, 30 p. c.	2 p. c.; 7 p. c.
Buttons	4,449,542	1,645,130	37.0	Metal, 45 p. c.; Silk, 50 p. c.; All other, 25 p. c.	9 p. c.; 13 p. c.; —12 p. c.
Calcium lights . . .	51,443	10,912	21.2	Metals, 45 p. c.	23.8 p. c.
Cardboard	959,145	116,410	12.1	15 p. c.	2.9 p. c.
Card-cutting and designing .	51,670	18,215	35.3	Metals, 45 p. c.	9.7 p. c.
Carpentering . . .	94,152,139	24,582,077	26.1	Paper, 15 p. c.; Metals, 40 p. c.; Manufactures of wood, 35 p. c.	—20.3 p. e.; 13.9 p. c.; 8.9 p. c.
Carpets:					
Rag	861,710	190,792	22.1	40 p. c.	17.9 p. c.
Other than rag (woollen) .	31,792,802	6,835,218	21.5	49.78 p. c.	28.28 p. c.
Wood	102,170	23,750	23.2	30 p. c.	6.8 p. c.
Carriage and wagon materials .	10,114,352	2,733,004	27.0	30 p. c.	7 p. c.
Carriages and sleds, children's .	1,677,776	462,852	27.6	35 p. c.	6.4 p. c.

Statement showing value of product, amount paid for hired labor, &c. — Continued.

Mechanical and manufacturing industries.	Value of product.	Amount paid for labor.	Percent. paid for labor.	(Tariff.) Rate of duty.	Excess of tariff over cost of labor.
Carriages and wagons	$64,951,617	$18,988,615	29.2	35 p. c.	5.8 p. c.
Cars, railroad, street, and repairs, not including steam-railroad companies	27,997,591	5,507,753	19.7	Metal, chief value, 45 p. c.	25.3 p. c.
Celluloid and celluloid goods	1,261,540	242,798	19.2	Wood, chief value, 35 p. c.	15.3 p. c.
Charcoal	975,540	390,697	40.0	Celluloid, 20 p. c.; goods, 35 p. c.	15.8 p. c.
Cheese and butter factory	25,742,510	1,546,495	6.0	Free.	
				Milk, 10 p. c.	4 p. c.
				Cheese, 4c. per lb. = 25.49 p. c.	19.49 p. c.
				Butter, 4c. per lb. = 18.40 p. c.	12.40 p. c.
				2c. per lb. = 6.5 p. c.	—.2 p. c.
Chocolate	1,302,153	82,258	6.3	Wood, 35 p. c.	6.4 p. c.
Cigar-moulds	111,820	32,020	28.6	Metal, 45 p. c.	16.4 p. c.
Cleansing and polishing preparations	500,280	91,455	18.3	Chemical, 25 p. c.	6.7 p. c.
				Polishing, 25 p. c.	6.7 p. c.
				Varnish, 40 p. c.	21.7 p. c.
Clock cases and materials	50,500	15,000	29.7	35 p. c.	5.3 p. c.
Clocks	4,110,267	1,622,693	39.5	30 p. c.	—9.5 p. c.
Cloth finishing	222,560	62,790	28.2	35 p. c.	6.8 p. c.
Clothing, horse	635,000	137,400	19.8	Cotton, 35 p. c.	15.2 p. c.
Clothing: Men's	209,548,460	45,940,353	21.9	Woollen, 50 p. c.	30.2 p. c.
				Cotton, 35 p. c.	13.1 p. c.
				Woollen, 60 p. c.	38.1 p. c.
				Linen, 40 p. c.	18.1 p. c.
Women's	32,004,794	6,661,005	20.8	Silk, 50 p. c.	28.1 p. c.
				Cotton, 35 p. c.	14.2 p. c.
				Woollen, 60 p. c.	39.2 p. c.
				Silk, 50 p. c.	29.2 p. c.
Coal-tar	466,800	65,500	14.0	Linen, 40 p. c.	19.2 p. c.
				20 p. c.	6.0 p. c.

Industry					
Coffee and spices, roasted, ground	22,924,894	1,370,699	6.0	Spices, ground, 5c. per lb. = 38 p. c.	24.0 p. c.
Coffins, burial cases, and undertaker's goods	8,157,700	1,895,805	23.2	Wood, 35 p. c.; Metal, 45 p. c.	11.8 p. c.; 21.8 p. c.
Coke	5,359,489	1,198,654	22.4	20 p. c.	− 2.4 p. c.
Collars and cuffs, paper	1,882,571	151,576	9.6	15 p. c.	5.4 p. c.
Combs	951,395	374,785	39.4	30 p. c.	− 9.4 p. c.
Confectionery	25,637,033	3,242,852	12.6	5c. per lb. = 38 p. c.; 10c. per lb. = 55 p. c. and 50 p. ¢.	25.4, 42.4, and 37.4 p. c.
Cooperage	$33,714,770	$8,992,603	26.7	35 p. c.	8.3 p. c.
Coppersmithing	2,087,773	520,302	24.9	45 p. c.	20.1 p. c.
Cordage and Twine	12,492,171	1,558,676	12.5	Tarred, 3c. per lb. = 28.8 p. c.; Untarred, 2¢. per lb. = 21 p. c.; All other, 3¢. per lb. = 28.8 p. c.	16.3 p. c.; 8.5 p. c.; 16.3 p. c.
Cordials and sirups	331,233	42,928	13.0	Cordials, $2 per gall. = 127 p. c.; Sirups, 35 p. c.	114.0 p. c.; 22.0 p. c.
Cork-cutting	1,566,555	232,846	14.9	25 p. c.	10.1 p. c.
Corsets	6,494,705	1,745,969	26.9	35 p. c.	8.1 p. c.
Cotton compressing	1,271,700	573,005	45.1	35 and 45 p. c.	
Cotton goods	210,950,383	45,614,419	21.6	Average, 38.3 p. c.; Thread, 50.2 p. c.	16.7 p. c.; 28.6 p. c.
Cotton-ties	262,351	38,069	14.5	25 p. c.	20.5 p. c.
Crucibles	1,445,641	284,169	19.7	25 p. c.	5.3 p. c.
Cutlery and edge tools	11,661,370	4,447,349	38.1	50 and 45 p. c.; metals, 45 p. c.	11.9 and 6.1 p. c.
Dentistry, mechanical	1,860,647	269,044	14.5	Teeth, 20 p. c.; metals, 45 p. c.	5.5 and 30.5 p. c.
Dentists' materials	860,708	237,729	27.6	Average, 45 p. c.	17.4 p. c.
Drain and sewer pipe	480,261	114,542	23.8	Earthen, 25 p. c.; Iron, 1c. per lb. = 32 p. c.	1.2 p. c.
Drugs and chemicals	38,173,658	4,157,163	10.9	37.1 p. c.	8.2 p. c.
Dyeing and cleaning	1,613,943	511,886	31.7	35 p. c.	26.2 p. c.
Dyeing and finishing textiles	32,297,420	6,474,364	20.0	Estimated, 35 p. c.	3.3 p. c.
Dyestuffs and extracts	5,253,038	512,097	9.7	Free. Extracts, 10 p. o.	15 p. c.
Electric lights	458,400	117,500	25.6	45 p. c.	19.4 p. c.
Electrical apparatus and supplies	1,074,388	224,758	20.9	45 p. c.	24.1 p. c.
Electroplating	1,975,700	620,848	31.4	45 p. c.	13.6 p. c.
Emery wheels	322,022	58,253	18.1	20 p. c.	1.9 p. c.
Enameled goods	321,511	41,906	13.0	45 p. c.	32 p. c.
Enameling	182,758	56,836	31.1	45 p. c.	13.9 p. c.
Engravers' materials	85,764	39,840	46.5	45 p. c.	− 1.5 p. c.
Engraving and die-sinking	1,180,165	419,646	35.6	45 p. c.	9.4 p. c.

Statement showing value of product, amount paid for hired labor, &c. — Continued.

Mechanical and manufacturing industries.	Each industry during census year (1880).			(Tariff.) Rate of duty.	Excess of tariff over cost of labor.
	Value of product.	Amount paid for labor.	Percent. paid for labor.		
Engraving:					
Steel	$2,998,616	$1,951,745	66.1	Steel plates, engraved, 25 p. c.	—40.1 p. c.
				Steel plates, prepared, 45 p. c.	—20.1 p. c.
Wood	734,728	333,590	45.4	Wood, engraved, 25 p. c.	—20.4 p. c.
				Wood, prepared, 35 p. c.	—10.4 p. c.
Envelopes	3,000,617	344,143	11.5	25 p. c.	13.5 p. c.
Explosives and fireworks	1,391,132	216,009	15.5	100 p. c.	84.5 p. c.
Fancy articles	2,817,230	1,036,672	36.8	Average, 38.4 p. c.	1.6 p. c.
Felt goods	3,619,652	439,760	12.1	Carpets, 40 p. c.	27.9 p. c.
				Woollens, 50 p. c.	37.9 p. c.
				Roofing, 20 p. c.	7.9 p. c.
Fertilizers	23,650,795	2,648,422	11.2	Free.	—11.2 p. c.
Files	2,486,533	957,412	38.5	35c., 75c., $1.50, and $2.50 per dozen; average, 56.7 p. c.	18.2 p. c.
Fire-arms	5,736,938	2,700,281	47.1	Shotgun barrels, 10 p. c.	—37.1 p. c.
				Breech-loading shotguns and pistols, 35 p.c.	—12.1 p. c.
				Muskets, rifles, and other fire-arms, 25 p. c.	—22.1 p. c.
Fire-extinguishers, chemical	204,623	84,750	71.4	45 p. c.	—26.4 p. c.
Flags and banners	119,600	27,375	22.9	Silk, 50 p. c.	27.1 p. c.
				Bunting, 62.8 p. c.	39.9 p. c.
				Cotton, 35 p. c.	12.1 p. c.
Flavoring extracts	1,195,637	129,343	10.8	50 p. c.	39.2 p. c.
Flax, dressed	1,310,231	266,420	20.5	$40 per ton = 7.7 p. c.	—12.8 p. o.
Flouring and grist-mill products	505,185,712	17,422,316	3.4	Wheat flour, 20 p. c.	16.4 p. c.
				Rye flour, ¼c. per lb. = 10 p. o.	6.4 p. c.
				Corn-meal, 10c. per bush. = 20.71 p. c.	17.3 p. c.
				Oat-meal, ½c. per lb. = 10 p. c.	6.4 p. c.
				Bran and other mill-feed, 20 p. c.	17.3 p. c.
Food preparations	2,493,224	318,253	12.8	20 p. c.	7.2 p. c.

Article				Tariff	
Foundery and machine-shop products	214,378,468	65,982,133	30.8	45 p. c.	14.2 p. c.
Foundery supplies	215,650	27,303	12.7	Sand, 10 p. c.; Pig-iron, $6.72 per ton; scrap iron, $6.72 ton = 37.2 p. c. Wood-moulds, 30 p. c.	—2.7 p. c.
Fruit-jar trimmings	485,503	104,501	21.5	Coal, 75c. per ton = 24.1 p. c. Rubber, 30 p. c.; metal, 45 p. c.	24.5 p. c. 17.3 p. c. 11.4 p. c. 8.5 and 23.5 p.c.
Fruits and vegetables, canned, preserved	17,599,576	2,679,960	15.2	35 p. c.	19.8 p. c.
Fuel, artificial	102,000	10,000	9.8	20 p. c.	10.2 p. c.
Furnishing goods, men's	11,506,857	2,644,155	23.0	Silk, 50 p. c. Woollen, 60 p. c. Linen, 40 p. c. Cotton, 35 p. c.	27 p. c. 17 p. c. 12 p. c. 7 p. c.
Furniture	63,037,902	20,383,794	30.0	India rubber manufactures, 30 p. c. Manufactured, 35 p. c. Silk reps, 50 p. c. Woollen reps, 55 p. c. Marble slabs, 50 p. c. Hair cloths, 23 p. c. Varnish, 40 p. c.	5 p. c. 20 p. c. 20 p. c. 25 p. c. 20 p. c. —7 p. c. 10 p. c.
Furniture, chairs	9,807,823	3,311,286	33.8	See articles for "Furniture," above	See Furniture.
Furs, dressed	8,238,712	1,389,284	16.9	20 p. c.	3.1 p. c.
Galvanizing	1,864,695	244,799	13.0	45 p. c.	32.0 p. c.
Gas and lamp fixtures	4,329,566	1,469,287	33.9	45 p. c.	11.1 p. c.
Gas machines and motors	1,334,091	397,108	29.8	45 p. c.	15.2 p. c.
Glass	21,154,571	9,144,100	43.2	Common window, average p. c., 68.5 p. c. Polished window, 25.2 p. c. Fluted or rough plate, 36.2 p. c. Plate glass, 85.8 p. c. Silvered glass, 28.8 p. c.	25.1 p. c. —18.0 p. c. —7.0 p. c. 42.6 p. c. 14.4 p.c.
Glass, cut, stained, ornamented	2,585,209	706,768	27.9	45 p. c.	17.1 p. c.
Gloves and mittens	7,379,605	1,655,695	22.4	Kid or leather, 50 p. c.	27.6 p. c.
Glucose	4,551,212	605,402	13.3	20 p. c.	6.7 p. c.
Glue	4,324,072	600,018	13.9	20 p. c.	6.1 p. c.
Gold and silver: Leaf and foil	1,614,040	410,647	25.4	Gold-leaf, $1.50 per pack = 30.8 p. c. Silver-leaf, 75c. per pack = 100.8 p. c.	5.4 p. c. 75.4 p. c.
Reduced and refined	9,548,188	178,696	1.9	Free. Crude, free.	—1.9 p. c.
Graphite	210,000	35,225	16.8	Manufactures of, 20 p. c.	3.2 p. c.

Statement showing value of product, amount paid for hired labor, &c. — Continued.

Mechanical and manufacturing industries.	Each industry during census year (1880).			(Tariff.) Rate of duty.	Excess of tariff over cost of labor.
	Value of product.	Amount paid for labor.	Percent. paid for labor.		
Grease and tallow	$13,730,013	$556,015	4.0	Grease, 10 p. c.; Tallow, 1c. per lb. = 13.5 p. c.	6.0 p. c.; 9.5 p. c.
Grindstones	164,555	57,040	30.9	$1.75 per ton = 14.4 p. c.	— 16.5 p. c.
Gunpowder	3,348,941	510,550	16.2	Valued 20c. or less per lb., 6c. per lb. = 37.6 { p. c. valued over 20c. per lb. 10c. per lb. }	12.4 p. c.
Hair-work	1,467,723	323,315	22.0	Hair-cloth, 30 p. c.; Hair, curled, 30 p. c.; Hair, seating, 23 p. c.; Bracelets, braids, curls, &c., 35 p. c.; Human hair, manufactured, 40 p. c.	8.0 p. c.; 8.0 p. c.; 1.0 p. c.; 13.0 p. c.; 18.0 p. c.
Hammocks	110,352	17,576	15.9	35 p. c.	19.1 p. c.
Hand-knit goods	446,354	137,720	30.9	Woollens, 55 p. c.	24.1 p. c.
Hand-stamps	318,618	82,895	26.0	Cottons, 40 p. c.; Metal, 45 p. c.; Rubber, 30 p. c.	9.1 p. c.; 19 p. c.; 4 p. c.
Handles, wooden	1,656,698	436,664	26.4	35 p. c.	8.6 p. c.
Hardware	22,653,693	6,846,913	30.2	45 p. c.	14.8 p. c.
Hardware, saddlery	3,651,021	960,432	26.3	35 p. c.	8.7 p. c.
Hat and cap materials	2,217,250	463,854	20.9	Silk, 50 p. c.; Cloth, 65.8 p. c.	29.1 p. c.; 44.9 p. c.
Hats and caps, not including wool hats	21,303,107	6,635,522	31.1	Leather and cloth, 35 p. c.; Metals, 45 p. c.; Straw, grass, &c., 35 p. c.; Silk, 50 p. c.	14.1 p. c.; 24.1 p. c.; — 1.1 p. c.; 18.1 p. c.
High explosives	2,453,088	164,864	6.7	(See Gunpowder.)	
Hones and whetstones	224,130	52,961	23.6	Free	— 23.6 p. c.
Hooks and eyes	370,078	83,321	23.9	45 p. c.	21.4 p. c.
Hosiery and knit goods	29,167,227	6,701,475	23.0	Cotton, 40 p. c.; Woollens, 55 p. c.	17 p. c.; 32 p. c.

Article				Tariff classification	Equiv. p. c.
House-furnishing goods	1,332,188	216,890	16.3	Earthenware, common, 25 p. c.	8.7 p. c.
				China, 55 p. c.	38.7 p. c.
				China, 60 p. c.	43.7 p. c.
				Cutlery, 45 p. c.	28.7 p. c.
				Glassware, 45 p. c.	28.7 p. c.
				Willowware, 30 p. c.	13.7 p. c.
				Wooden-ware, 35 p. c.	18.7 p. c.
				Linens, 40 p. c.	23.7 p. c.
				Cottons, 35 p. c.	18.7 p. c.
				Metals, 45 p. c.	28.7 p. c.
				Chemicals, 25 p. c.; metals, 45 p. c.	19.1 p. c.
				30 p. c.	15.9 p. c.
Ice, artificial	544,763	140,885	25.9	35 p. c.	—.9 p. c.
Ink	1,629,413	230,284	14.1	Average, 40.9 p. c.	22.2 p. c.
Instruments, professional and scientific	1,639,094	568,751	35.9	2½c. per lb. = 45 p. c.	25.3 p. c.
Iron and steel	296,557,685	55,476,785	18.7	45 p. c.	24.1 p. c.
Iron bolts, nuts, washers, and rivets	10,073,330	1,981,300	19.7	2½c. per lb. = 45 p. c.	24.5 p. c.
Iron doors and shutters	495,060	103,269	20.9	Cut, 1½c. per lb. = 31.7 p. c.	9.4 p. c.
Iron forgings	6,492,028	1,329,151	20.5	2c. per lb. = 72.2 p. c.	49.9 p. c.
Iron nails and spikes, cut, wrought	6,529,240	1,255,171	22.3	2½c. per lb. = 42 p. c.	28.5 p. c.
Iron pipe, wrought	13,292,162	1,788,258	13.5	45 p. c.	16.6 p. c.
Iron railing, wrought	1,300,549	369,903	28.4	45 p. c.	22.5 p. c.
Iron work, architectural and ornamental	2,109,537	474,711	22.5	Billiard and bagatelle balls, dice, &c., 50 p. c.	21.5 p. c.
Ivory and bone work	1,454,901	414,701	28.5	Other ivory work, 30 p. c.	1.5 p. c.
				40 p. c.	5.5 p. c.
Japanning	190,080	65,562	34.5	25 p. c.	— 4.0 p. c.
Jewelry	22,201,621	6,441,688	29.0	Wood, 35 p. c.	— 3.7 p. c.
Jewelry and instrument cases	131,670	51,000	38.7	Metal, 45 p. c.	6.3 p. c.
				Silk, 50 p. c.	11.3 p. c.
Jute and jute goods	696,982	141,979	20.4	Jute butts, $5 per ton = 15.6 p. c.	— 4.8 p. c.
				Jute yarns, 35 p. c.	14.6 p. c.
				Burlaps, oilcloth foundation, and manufactures of, not otherwise specified, 40 p. c.	19.6 p. c.
Kaolin and ground earths	1,455,757	310,909	21.4	$3 per ton = 32.7 p. c.	11.3 p. c.
				Ochres, ¼c. per lb. = 39.5 p. c.	18.1 p. c.
Kindling wool	2,480,953	526,861	21.2	35 p. c.	13.8 p. c.
Labels and tags	865,825	149,268	17.2	Paper, 15 p. c.	— 2.2 p. c.
				Metal, 45 p. c.	27.8 p. c.
Lamps and reflectors	3,357,829	742,423	22.1	Cotton or rubber, 35 p. c.	17.8 p. c.
				45 p. c.	22.9 p. c.

Statement showing value of product, amount paid for hired labor, &c. — Continued.

Mechanical and manufacturing industries.	Each industry during census year (1880).			(Tariff.) Rate of duty.	Excess of tariff over cost of labor.
	Value of product.	Amount paid for labor.	Percent. paid for labor.		
Lapidary work	$544,089	$142,075	26.1	25 p. c. = 13.9 p. c.	— 1.1 p. c.
Lard, refined	23,135,702	546,258	2.4	2c. per lb. = 13.9 p. c.	11.5 p. c.
Lasts	765,296	308,975	40.4	30 p. c.	— 10.4 p. c.
Lead, bar, pipe, sheet, and shot	5,600,671	316,363	5.6	Bar, 2c. per lb. = 63.5 p. c.	57.9 p. c.
				Pipe, sheet, and shot, 3c. per lb. = 62.7 p. c.	57.1 p. c.
Leather:					
Board	689,300	121,015	17.6	30 p. c.	12.4 p. c.
Curried	71,351,297	4,845,413	6.8	20 p. c.	13.2 p. c.
Dressed skins	15,309,311	2,441,372	15.9	20 p. c.	4.1 p. c.
Goods	2,020,343	459,318	22.7	30 p. c.	7.3 p. c.
Morocco (see Dressed skins)	. .	.		10 p. c.	
Patent and enamelled	166,000	12,800	7.7	30 p. c.	22.3 p. c.
Tanned	113,348,336	9,204,243	8.1	20 p. c.	11.9 p. c.
Lightning rods	801,192	73,718	9.2	45 p. c.	35.8 p. c.
Lime and cement	5,772,318	1,579,313	27.4	Lime, 10 p. c.	— 17.4 p. c.
				Cement, 20 p. c.	— 7.4 p. c.
Linen goods	602,451	124,046	20.6	40 p. c.	19.4 p. c.
Liquors:					
Distilled	41,063,663	2,663,967	6.5	$2 gall. = Cordials, 127 p. c.	120.5 p. c.
				Brandy, 83.3 p. c.	66.8 p. o.
				Spirits from grain, 302.4 p. c.	795.9 p. c.
				Spirits from other materials, 322.9 p. c.	
Malt	101,058,385	12,196,053	12.1	Bulk, 20c. per gall. = 56.8 p. c.	231.4 p. c.
				In bottles, 35c. per gall. = 39.3 p. c.	44.7 p. c.
				Champagne, $1.75, $3.50, and $7 per doz. = 56.2 p. c.	27.2 p. c.
Vinous	2,169,193	216,550	10.0	Still wines, in bulk, 50c. per gal. = 78.8 p. c.	46.2 p. c.
					68.8 p. c.
				Same, in bottles, $1.60 per doz. = 28.7 p. c.	18.7 p. c.

					Average about 16 p. c.
Lithographing	6,912,338	2,307,302	33.4	Stone, 20 p. c. . . .	— 13.4 p. c.
Lock and gun smithing . .	1,317,810	368,967	28.0	Metal, 45 p. c. . . .	11.6 p. c.
Looking-glass and picture-frames .	2,696,219	2,471,105	25.8	45 p. c. (see Firearms) . .	17.0 p. c.
				35 p. c.	9.2 p. c.
Lumber: Planed . . .	36,803,356	5,890,724	16.0	In addition to duty on lumber if planed on one side, 50c. per M ft. . Planed on two sides, $1 per M ft . Planed on one side and tongued and grooved, $1 per M ft . Planed on both sides and tongued and grooved, $1.50 per M ft .	
Sawed	233,268,729	31,845,974	13.7	Hemlock, whitewood, sycamore, and basswood, $1 per M ft. = 11.4 p. c. .	— 2.3 p. 3.
				All other, $2 per M ft. = 14.6 p. c. .	0.9 p. c.
Malt	18,273,102	1,004,548	5.5	20c. per bush. = 24.1 p. c. . .	18.6 p. c.
Mantels, slate, marble, marbleized	1,030,660	318,009	30.4	Slate, 30 p. c. . . .	— 0.4 p. c.
				Marble, 50 p. c. . . .	19.6 p. c.
Marble and stone work . .	31,415,150	10,238,885	32.6	Marble, 65c. per cubic ft. = 90.7. p. c.	58.1 P. e.
				Marble, manufactures of, 50 p. c. .	17.4 p. c.
				Stone, dressed, $1 per ton = 22.1 p. c.	— 10.5 p. c.
				Stone, manufactures of, 20 p. c. .	— 12.6 p. c.
Masonry, brick and stone . .	20,586,553	6,880,866	33.4	Brick, 20 p. c. (see Stone, above) (see Lime and cement)	— 13.4 p. c.
Matches	4,668,446	535,911	11.5	35 p. c.	23.5 p. e.
Mats and matting . . .	439,370	125,129	28.5	20 p. c.	— 8.5 p. c.
Mattresses and spring beds . .	5,288,234	808,325	16.4	Mattresses, 30 p. c. . .	13.6 p. c.
Millinery and lace goods . .	9,577,840	1,661,044	17.3	Steel wire, average, 38 p. c. .	21.6 p. c.
				Laces, 40 p. c. . . .	22.7 p. c.
				Silks, 50 p. c. . . .	32.7 p. c.
				Feathers and flowers, 50 p. c. .	32.7 p. c.
				Straw goods, 30 p. c. . .	12.7 p. c.
Millstones	356,519	96,534	27.2	20 p. c.	— 7.2 p. c.
Mineral and soda waters . .	4,741,709	1,065,633	22.5	30 p. c.	7.3 p. c.
Mirrors	304,000	42,900	14.1	30 p. c.	16.9 p. c.
Mixed textiles	66,221,703	13,316,753	20.1	Dutiable according to material, from 35 to 60 p. c. . . .	14.9 to 39.9 p.o.
Models and patterns . . .	908,830	389,837	42.9	Wood, 35 p. c. . . .	— 7.2 p. c.
				Metals, 45 p. c. . . .	2.1 p. c.
Mucilage and paste . . .	16,700	3,090	18.5	20 p. c.	1.5 p. c.
Musical instruments, materials .	853,746	293,062	34.3	25 p. c., 45 p. c. . .	—9.3+10.7 p.c.

Statement showing value of product, amount paid for hired labor, &c. — Continued.

Mechanical and manufacturing industries.	Each industry during census year (1880). Value of product.	Amount paid for labor.	Percent, paid for labor.	(Tariff.) Rate of duty.	Excess of tariff over cost of labor.
Musical instruments, organs, and materials	$6,136,472	$2,142,539	34.9	25 p. c., 45 p. c.	—9.9+10.1 p.c.
Musical instruments, pianos, and materials	12,264,521	4,663,193	38.0	25 p. c., 45 p. c.	—13.0+7.0 p.c.
Needles and pins	1,378,023	392,214	28.5	Needles, 25 p. c. Pins, 30 p. c.	—3.5 p. c. 1.5 p. c.
Nets and seines	291,765	54,112	18.5	25 p. c.	6.5 p. c.
Oil:					
Castor	653,900	44,714	6.8	80c. per gall. = 62.1 p. c.	55.3 p. c.
Cotton-seed and cake	7,690,921	880,836	11.5	25c. per gall. = 20 p. c.	8.5 p. c.
Essential	248,858	24,030	9.7	25 p. c.	15.3 p. c.
Illuminating, not including petroleum refined	510,000	20,950	4.1	25 p. c.	20.9 p. c.
Lard	4,721,066	161,672	3.4	25 p. c.	21.6 p. c.
Linseed	15,393,812	681,677	4.4	25c. per gall. = 68.8 p. c.	56.4 p. c.
Lubricating	2,925,501	208,145	7.1	25 p. c.	17.9 p. c.
Neatsfoot	259,086	16,554	6.4	25 p. c.	18.6 p. c.
Resin	238,471	14,590	6.1	25 p. c.	18.9 p. c.
Oilcloth:					
Enamelled	1,062,000	116,627	11.0	40 p. c.	29.0 p. c.
Floor	4,762,587	733,235	15.4	40 p. c.	24.6 p. c.
Oleomargarine	6,892,939	212,952	3.1	As butter, 4c, per lb. = 18.4 p. c.	15.3 p. c.
Painting and paper-hanging	22,457,560	7,920,866	35.3	Paints, 33 p. c.; hangings, 25 p. c.	—2.3+10.3 p.c.
Paints	23,330,767	2,132,255	9.1	33 p. c.	23.9 p. c.
Paper	55,109,914	8,525,355	15.5	Printing, unsized, 15 p. c. Printing, sized, 20 p. c. Common, 15 p. c. Writing, 25 p. c.	—0.5 p. c. 4.5 p. c. —0.5 p. c. 9.5 p. c.
Paper-hangings	6,267,303	874,921	14.0	25 p. c.	11.0 p. c.
Paper patterns	512,550	40,638	7.9	15 p. c.	7.1 p. c.

Item				Rate	
Patent medicines and compounds	14,682,494	1,651,596	11.2	50 p. c.	38.8 p. c.
Paving materials	1,024,243	244,339	23.9	20 p. c.	—3.9 p. c.
Pencils, lead	279,427	102,233	33.6	50c. gross and 30 p. c. = 54.5 p. c.	17.9 p. c.
Pens: Gold	533,061	172,207	32.3	45 p. c.	10.7 p. c.
Steel	164,000	88,500	54.0	12c. per gross = 39.6 p. c.	—14.4 p. c.
Perfumery and cosmetics	2,203,004	238,259	10.8	Cologne, $2 per gall. and 50 p. c. = 59.2 p. c.	48.4 p. c.
				Other perfumery, 50 p. c.	39.2 p. c.
				46 lt.	5.4 p. c.
Photographing apparatus	104,305	41,314	39.6	46 lt.	—4.5 p. c.
Photographing	5,935,311	1,751,118	29.5	Photographs, 25 p. c.	20.5 p. c.
				Silk cases, 50 p. c.	15.5 p. c.
				Metal cases, 45 p. c.	17.2 p. c.
Photographing materials	142,000	25,310	17.8	Chemicals, 35 p. c.	24.2 p. c.
Pickles, preserves, and sauces	2,407,342	250,454	10.8	35 p. c.	34.0 p. c.
Pipes, tobacco	628,688	226,306	36.0	70 p. c.	6.5 p. c.
Plated and britannia ware	8,556,181	2,453,361	28.5	35 p. c.	18.7 p. c.
Plumbing and gas-fitting	18,133,250	4,770,389	26.3	Metal, 45 p. c.; earthenware, 25 p. c.	7.6 p. c.
Pocketbooks	1,769,036	464,947	27.4	35 p. o.	9.7 p. c.
Postal cards	190,000	10,000	5.3	15 p. c.	—8.6 p. c.
Printing and publishing	90,780,341	30,531,657	33.6	25 p. c.	—8.5 p. c.
Printing materials	421,316	98,878	23.5	Paper, unsized, 15 p. c.	—3.5 p. c.
				Paper, sized, 20 p. c.	1.5 p. c.
				Type, 25 p. c.	6.5 p. c.
				Ink, 30 p. c.	17.1 p. c.
Pumps, not including steam-pumps	3,644,631	652,749	17.9	Wood, 35 p. c.	27.1 p. c.
				Metal, 45 p. c.	8.2 p. c.
Racking hose	5,512	1,200	21.8	30 p. c.	5.6 p. c.
Refrigerators	1,739,731	423,680	24.4	30 p. c.	
Regalia and society banners and emblems	815,638	174,097	21.3	25 p. c.	3.7 p. c.
Registers, car-fare	6,600	4,875	73.9	45 p. c.	—28.9 p. c.
Rice cleaning and polishing	3,133,324	110,467	3.5	Rice, cleaned, 2½c. per lb. = 95.7 p. c.	92.2 p. c.
				Rice, uncleaned, 1½c. per lb. = 78.8 p. c.	75.3 p. c.
				Paddy, 1½c. per lb. = 102.1 p. c.	96.6 p. c.
Roofing and roofing materials	6,227,284	1,411,133	22.7	Tin-plate, 1c. per lb. = 27.2 p. c.	4.5 p. c.
				Sheet-iron, 49.5 p. c.	26.8 p. c.
				Sheet-iron, 48.9 p. c.	26.2 p. c.
				Sheet-iron, 40.2 p. c.	17.5 p. c.
				Roofing, felt, 20 p. c.	—2.7 p. c.
				Pitch, 20 p. c.	2.7 p. c.
Rubber and elastic goods	13,751,724	2,295,972	16.7	Wholly of rubber, 25 p. c.	8.3 p. c.
				Boots and shoes, 25 p. c.	8.3 p. c.
				Manufactures of, 30 p. c.	13.3 p. c.

Statement showing value of product, amount paid for hired labor, &c. — Continued.

Mechanical and manufacturing industries.	Each industry during census year (1880).			(Tariff.) Rate of duty.	Excess of tariff over cost of labor.
	Value of product.	Amount paid for labor.	Percent. paid for labor.		
Rubber, vulcanized	$767,200	$154,700	20.2	25 p. c.	4.8 p. o.
Rules, ivory and wood	66,200	19,974	30.2	30 p. c.	0.0 p. c.
Saddlery and harness	38,081,643	7,997,752	21.0	35 p. c.	14.0 p. c.
Safes, doors, and vaults, fire-proof	3,352,396	1,096,504	32.7	45 p. c.	12.3 p. c.
Salt	4,929,566	1,260,023	26.1	8c. per 100 lbs. = 73.3 p. c.	47.2 p. c.
Salt, ground	361,656	44,997	12.4	12c. per 100 lbs. = 36.6 p. c.	10.5 p. c.
Sand and emery paper and cloth	262,374	30,970	11.8	20 p. c.	8.2 p. c.
Sash, doors, and blinds	36,621,325	8,540,930	23.3	35 p. c.	11.7 p. c.
Saws	3,943,105	1,226,370	31.1	40 p. c.	8.9 p. o.
Scales and balances	3,252,460	783,019	24.1	45 p. c.	20.9 p. c.
Screws	2,184,532	450,542	20.9	6, 8, 10, and 12c. per lb., according to size; average, 53.9 p. c.	33.0 p. o.
Sewing-machine cases	2,064,837	683,338	33.1	35 p. c.	1.9 p. c.
Sewing-machines and attachments	13,863,188	4,636,099	33.4	45 p. c.	11.6 p. c.
Shingles, split	47,952	11,394	23.8	35c. per M = 13 p. c.	—10.8 p. c.
Ship-building	36,800,327	12,713,813	34.5	50 p. c.	15.5 p. c.
Shirts	20,130,031	5,403,096	26.8	35 p. c.	8.2 p. c.
Shoddy	4,989,615	400,326	8.0	10c. per lb. = 23 p. c.	15.0 p. c.
Show-cases	1,172,172	329,230	28.1	Wood, 35 p. c.; metal, 45 p. c.	6.9 and 16.9 p. c.
Silk and silk goods	41,033,045	9,146,705	22.3	50 p. o.	27.7 p. c.
Silversmithing	263,931	76,640	29.0	45 p. c.	16.0 p. c.
Silverware	2,253,630	675,943	30.0	45 p. c.	15.0 p. c.
Slaughtering and meat-packing, not including retail butchering establishments	303,562,413	10,508,530	3.5	Pork, 1c. per lb. = 11.2 p. c. Bacon and hams, 2c. per lb. = 10.2 p. c. Beef, 1c. per lb. = 12.7 p. c. Tallow, 1c. per lb. = 13.5 p. c. Lard, 2c. per lb. = 13.9 p. c.	7.7 p. c. 6.7 p. c. 9.2 p. o. 10.0 p. o. 10.4 p. o.
Smelting and refining	8,411,100	158,300	1.9	Gold and silver ores, free; copper, 2½c. per lb. = 24.6 p. c. Iron, 75c. per ton = 28.4 p. c.	22.7 p. o. 26.5 p. o.

Article				Details	
Soaps and candles	26,552,627	2,219,513	8.4	Fancy soap, 15c. per lb. = 28.4 p. c.	20.0 p. c.
				Soft soap, 20 p. c.	11.6 p. c.
				Candles, 20 p. c.	11.6 p. c.
Soda-water apparatus	1,075,560	169,235	15.7	Metal, 45 p. c.	19.3 p. c.
				Marble, 50 p. c.	31.3 p. c.
Spectacles and eye-glasses	1,182,142	450,897	38.1	45 p. c.	6.9 p. c.
Sporting goods	1,556,258	411,854	26.5	Manufactures of metal, 45 p. c.	18.5 p. c.
				Manufactures of wood, 35 p. c.	8.5 p. c.
				Manufactures of leather, 30 p. c.	3.5 p. c.
				Manufactures of ivory, 50 p. c.	23.5 p. c.
Springs, steel, car, and carriage	3,654,862	639,412	19.1	Cards, playing, 100 p. c.	74.5 p. c.
Stamped-ware	3,512,423	868,043	24.7	45 p. c.	25.9 p. c.
Starch	7,477,742	919,197	12.3	45 p. c.	20.3 p. c.
				Potato or corn, 2c. per lb. = 71.6 p. c.	59.3 p. c.
				All other, 2½c. per lb. = 72.2 p. c.	59.9 p. c.
Stationery goods	5,898,322	1,159,893	19.7	Books, papers, &c. 25 p. c.	5.3 p. c.
				Writing paper, 25 p. c.	5.3 p. c.
				Manufactures of paper, 15 p. c.	—4.7 p. c.
				Manufactures of glass, 45 p. c.	25.3 p. c.
				Manufactures of metal, 45 p. c.	25.3 p. c.
				Manufactures of rubber, 30 p. c.	0.3 p. c.
				Manufactures of leather, 30 p. c.	10.3 p. c.
				Manufactures of wood, 35 p. c.	15.3 p. c.
Steam-fittings, heating apparatus	5,127,842	1,305,739	25.5	45 p. c.	19.5 p. c.
Stencils and brands	472,514	139,639	29.6	45 p. c.	15.4 p. c.
Stereotyping and electrotyping	724,640	312,208	43.1	25 p. c.	18.1 p. c.
Stone and earthenware	7,942,729	3,279,535	41.3	Brown and common, 25 p. c.	—16.3 p. c.
				China, plain, 55 p. c.	13.7 p. c.
				China, ornamented, 60 p. c.	18.7 p. c.
Straw goods	9,345,750	2,556,197	27.4	30 p. c.	2.6 p. c.
Sugar and molasses, beet	282,572	-62,271	22.0	(See below.)	
Sugar and molasses, refined	155,484,915	2,875,032	1.8	Sugar not above 75°, by the polariscope, 1.4c. per lb., and .04c. per lb. for every degree additional — average about 46 p.c.	44.2 p. c.
				Molasses not above 56°, 4c. per gall. = 15.9 p. c.	
Surgical appliances	906,303	265,372	29.3	Above 56°, 8c. per gall. = 35.7 p. c.	14.1 p. c.
				35 p. c.	33.9 p. c.
Tar and turpentine, not including farm products	5,876,983	1,623,061	27.6	20 p. c.	5.7 p. c.
Taxidermy	82,500	22,000	26.7	Free ?	—7.6 p. e.

Statement showing value of product, amount paid for hired labor, &c. — Concluded.

Mechanical and manufacturing industries.	Each industry during census year (1880).			(Tariff.) Rate of duty.	Excess of tariff over cost of labor.
	Value of product.	Amount paid for labor.	Percent. paid for labor.		
Telegraph and telephone apparatus	$1,580,648	$159,406	29.0	45 p. c.	16.0 p. c.
Terra-cotta ware	554,343	206,650	37.3	25 p. c.	— 12.3 p. c.
Thread, linen	1,200,000	280,000	21.7	40 p. c.	18.3 p. c.
Tinware, copperware, and sheet-iron ware	48,096,038	10,722,974	22.3	45 p. c.	22.7 p. c.
Tinfoil	416,849	100,673	24.2	45 p. c.	20.8 p. c.
Tobacco, chewing, smoking, snuff	52,793,056	6,419,024	12.2	Leaf, 33c. per lb. = 65.2 p. c.,	53.0 p. c.
				Manufactured, 40c. per lb. = 182.0 p. c.	169.8 p. c.
				Snuff, 50c. per lb. = 119.2 p. c.	107.2 p. c.
Tobacco, cigars, and cigarettes	63,979,575	18,464,562	28.9	$2.50 per lb. and 25 p. c. = 89.4 p. c.	60.5 p. c.
Tobacco, stemming	1,879,535	170,871	9.0	30 p. c.	21.0 p. c.
Tools	4,236,568	1,489,531	35.2	45 p. c.	9.8 p. c.
Toys and games	1,562,513	512,746	32.8	35 p. c.	2.2 p. c.
Trunks and valises	7,252,470	1,786,546	24.6	35 p. c.	10.4 p. c.
Type founding	2,330,298	958,698	41.1	25 p. c.	— 16.1 p. c.
Umbrellas and canes	6,917,463	1,158,682	16.8	Silk or alpaca umbrellas, 50 p. c.	33.2 p. c.
				All other umbrellas, 40 p. c.	23.2 p. c.
				Canes, 35 p. c.	18.2 p. c.
Upholstering	7,158,893	1,353,334	18.9	Average, 35 p. c.	16.1 p. c.
Upholstering materials	1,837,705	523,417	28.5	Average, 35 p. c.	6.5 p. c.
Varnish	5,721,174	366,716	6.4	40 p. c.	33.6 p. c.
Vault-lights and ventilators	273,395	66,204	24.2	45 p. c.	21.0 p. c.
Veneerings	292,205	35,730	12.2	20 p. c.	7.8 p. c.
Vinegar	3,418,038	413,451	12.1	7½c. per gall. = 37.6 p. c.	25.5 p. c.
Washing-machines, clothes wringers	1,182,714	176,287	14.9	35 p. c.	20.1 p. c.
Watch and clock materials	300,195	86,050	28.7	35 p. c.	— 3.7 p. c.
Watch and clock repairing	2,712,819	866,496	32.0	25 p. c.	— 7.0 p. c.
Watch cases	4,589,314	976,041	21.3	25 p. c.	3.7 p. c.

Article	Value	%	Rates	
Watches	3,271,244	52.3	25 p. c.	—27.3 p. c.
Whalebone and rattan	526,777	14.2	Whalebone, 30 p. c.	15.8 p. c.
			Rattans, 10 p. c.	—4.2 p. c.
Wheelbarrows	227,392	31.9	Wood, 35 p. c.	3.1 p. c.
			Metal, 45 p. c.	13.1 p. c.
Wheelwrighting	18,892,858	26.9	35 p. c.	8.1 p. c.
Whips	1,698,633	24.4	35 p. c.	10.6 p. c.
Windmills	1,010,542	24.2	35 p. c.	10.8 p. c.
Window blinds and sash	2,826,518	17.0	35 p. c.	18.0 p. c.
Wire	10,836,600	18.3	Wire, 1¼, 2, 2½, and 3c. per lb.; galvanized, 2, 2½, 3, and 3½c. per lb. = 27.1 p. c., Covered with cotton, 5½, 6, 6½, and 7c. per lb. = 12.2 p. c.	8.8 p. c.
Wire-work	9,127,818	18.0	Iron wire-rope, 2½, 3, 3½, and 4c. per lb. = 72.2 p. c.	—6.2 p. c.
			Steel wire-rope, &c., 3¾, 4, 4½, and 5c. per lb. = 44.3 p. c.	63.5 p. c.
Wood preserving	101,110	14.6	20 p. c.	25.6 p. c.
Wood-pulp	2,256,946	19.7	10 p. c.	5.4 p. c.
Wood, turned and carved	6,770,119	31.7	35 p. c.	—9.7 p. c.
Woodenware	5,235,474	29.4	35 p. c.	3.3 p. c.
Wool hats	8,516,563	22.2	Flannels, blankets, hats of wool, knit-goods, balmorals, yarns, and other manufactures of—10c. per lb. and 35 p. c., 12c. per lb. and 35 p. c. = 62.8 p. c.; 18c. per lb. and 35 p. c. = 68.4 p. c.; 24c. per lb. and 35 p. c. = 67.9 p. c.; 35c. per lb. and 35 p. c. = 62.1 p. c.	5.6 p. c.
Woollen goods	160,606,721	16.1	Women's and children's dress goods—5c. per yard and 35 p. c. = 63.5 p. c.; 7c. per yard and 40 p. c., 9c. per yard and 40 p. c. = 64.9 p. c.; 35c. per yard and 40 p. c. = 63.7 p. c.; average, 64 p. c. Cloth—35c. per lb. and 35 p. c., 35c. per lb. and 40 p. c. = 65.8 p. c.	48.5 p. c.
Worsted goods	33,549,942	16.9	45c. per sq. yard and 35 p. c., 30c. per sq. yard and 30 p. c., 25c. per sq. yard and 30 p. c., 20c. per sq. yard and 30 p. c., 16c. per sq. yard and 30 p. c., 12c. per sq. yard and 30 p. c., 8c. per sq. yard and 30 p. c. = 49.8 p. c. Carpets—	49.5 p. c.
	5,683,027			49.3 p. c.
Zinc	2,725,165	24.5	Block or pigs, 1½c. per lb. = 39.1 p. c. Sheets, 2½c. per lb. = 58.3 p. c. Manufactures of, 45 p. c.	33.3 p. c. / 14.6 p. c. / 33.8 p. c. / 20.5 p. c.